The Complete Idiot's Reference Card

(You Mean I Spent All That Time Writing This Book, and You're Not Going to Read It?)

Function Keys

Key	Name	Action
F1	Help	Activate the Help system.
F2	Edit	Switch to EDIT mode for editing cell entries.
F3	Name	Display a list of names to choose from.
F4	Abs	Cycle the cell references in formulas through absolute, mixed, and relative.
F5	Goto	Move the cell pointer to the specified location.
F6	Window	Move the cell pointer between windows.
F7	Query	Repeat the last Data Query command.
F8	Table	Repeat the last Data Table command.
F9	Calc	Recalculate all worksheet formulas.
F10	Graph	Display the current graph.

Cell Pointer Movement Keys:

Press...	To move the cell pointer...
↑, ↓	Up or down one row.
←, →	Left or right one column.
PgUp	Up one screen.
PgDn	Down one screen.
Ctrl+→ or Tab	Right one screen.
← or Shift+Tab	Left one screen.
Home	To cell A1 in the current worksheet.
End, Home	To the lower right corner of the worksheet's active area.
Ctrl+PgUp	To the next worksheet.
Ctrl+PgDn	To the previous worksheet.
Ctrl+Home	To cell A1 in worksheet A.
End, any arrow key	In the indicated direction, until it reaches the first data-containing cell that is next to an empty cell.

alpha books

Table Prefix Characters:

Prefix character	Effect
'	Left-aligns label in cell.
"	Right-aligns label in cell.
^	Centers label in cell.
\	Repeats label across cell.

The Most Frequently Used SmartIcons and Their Menu or Keyboard Equivalents:

SmartIcons	Equivalent menu command	Description
	/File Save	Save the current worksheet file on disk.
	/File Retrieve	Retrieve a worksheet file from disk, replacing the current worksheet file in memory.
	/File Open	Retrieve a worksheet file from disk without replacing the current worksheet file in memory.
	/Worksheet Window Perspective	Switch perspective view, which lets you view three worksheets on-screen at once, on or off.
	none	Sum the values in a range.
	F10	Display the current graph or a QuickGraph.
	:Graph Add	Add the current graph to the worksheet.
	:Print Go	Print the current range.
	:Print Preview	Preview the current print range.
	:Format Bold	Add or remove boldface.
	:Format Italics	Add or remove italics.
	:Format Underline	Add or remove underlining.
	F1	Activate the Help system.
	none	Display other SmartIcon sets.

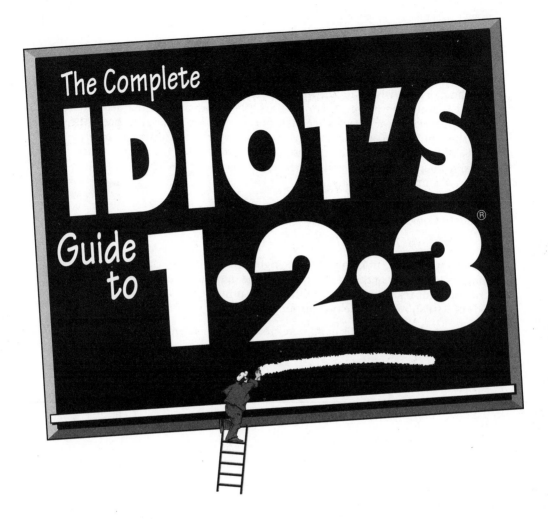

by Peter Aitken

alpha books

A Division of Prentice Hall Computer Publishing
11711 North College Avenue, Carmel, Indiana 46032 USA

©1993 Alpha Books

International Standard Book Number: 1-56761-285-7
Library of Congress Catalog Card Number: 93-71732

95 94 93   8 7 6 5 4 3 2 1

Interpretation of the printing code: the rightmost number of the first series of numbers is the year of the book's printing; the rightmost number of the second series of numbers is the number of the book's printing. For example, a printing code of 93-1 shows that the first printing of the book occurred in 1993.

Screen reproductions in this book were created by means of the program Collage Plus from Inner Media, Inc., Hollis, NH.

Printed in the United States of America

Publisher
Marie Butler-Knight

Associate Publisher
Lisa A. Bucki

Managing Editor
Elizabeth Keaffaber

Development Editor
Seta Frantz

Acquisitions Manager
Stephen R. Poland

Production Editor
Michelle Shaw

Imprint Manager
Scott Cook

Cover Designer
Scott Cook

Designer
Amy Peppler-Adams, Roger Morgan

Illustrations
Steve Vanderbosch

Indexer
Jeanne Clark

Production Team
*Diana Bigham, Katy Bodenmiller, Brad Chinn, Scott Cook,
Tim Cox, Meshell Dinn, Mark Enochs, Tom Loveman,
Roger Morgan, Beth Rago, Carrie Roth, Greg Simsic*

*Special thanks to Kelly Oliver for ensuring the
technical accuracy of this book.*

Contents at a Glance

Contents

Introduction

This book is called an *Idiot's Guide*, but it's not really for idiots. It's for folks like you—intelligent, capable people who can organize a business presentation, balance a checkbook, and even program a VCR. Well, maybe you can't program a VCR—I can't, either (I get my son to do it). Even so, you were doing just fine until you bumped into a computer and a program called Lotus 1-2-3.

You bought this book in the hopes that it will help you learn how to use 1-2-3. You don't want to become a PC guru or a 1-2-3 wizard, you simply want to learn enough so you can get some useful work done. You've made a good choice!

Why Do You Need This Book?

There are dozens of books on Lotus 1-2-3 available, so why do you need this one? For starters, I don't assume that you know anything about computers or Lotus 1-2-3. Every term, instruction, and task is fully explained so you know exactly what's going on. Better still, they are explained in English! There's no need to know computerese before reading this book.

Furthermore, I have taken a very practical approach in deciding what to cover and what to skip. Rather than wasting your time with lots of obscure program details that you'll never use, I have concentrated on those things you'll need most often. You won't be a 1-2-3 expert after reading the book, but then you don't want to be! You will, however, be able to use 1-2-3 for your daily work.

Finally, I have tried to make the book entertaining and easy to read. I know that the terms "entertaining" and "computer book" usually do not go together, but I think this book is an exception. By not taking things too seriously, and poking a bit of fun here and there, I hope to have presented a rather dry subject in a manner you'll find more enjoyable than that of other computer books.

How Do You Use This Book?

You can use this book several ways. If you like (and if you have insomnia) you can read it from start to finish. This is not really necessary, however. The book is organized so you can use the Table of Contents and the Index to find a particular item quickly. Keep the book next to your computer so you can refer to it as needed while you are working.

If you're a real computer novice, however, I suggest that you start by reading through Part One, preferably while sitting at your computer so you can try things out as you read. These 8 chapters will teach you the basics of 1-2-3, enough so you can start doing some real work. Then you can refer to other parts of the book as needed.

Two Flavors of 1-2-3

Lotus 1-2-3 comes in two flavors, or *versions*. One is called Release 3.4, and the other is called Release 2.4. In most ways they are similar or identical, and information in the book that applies to one will apply equally to the other. There are some differences, however. In these cases, the main text of the book applies to Release 3.4, and the Release 2.4 differences are pointed out in specially-marked sections.

What's in the Book?

The contents of the book are organized into 20 chapters in five parts. Within each chapter, the book follows certain conventions to present information in a clear and consistent manner. When you need to type something, it will appear like this:

Type Me In

Any individual keys you need to press are in darker type, like this: Press the **Enter** key. Sometimes you need to press two keys at once; they are given with a plus (+) sign between them. For example, if you see **Ctrl+C**, it means to press and hold the **Ctrl** key, press the C key, then release both keys. You don't need to type the + key.

Throughout the book, a number of special elements are used to help speed the learning process and make the book easier to read:

Put It to Work
Real-life ways you can use 1-2-3.

By the Way . . .
Generally worthless but occasionally humorous comments from me.

Plain English definitions of computer terms. Learn these and you too can "Speak Like a Geek!"

Background technical information that you should read only if you are interested. Not necessary for learning how to use 1-2-3.

Tips on the easiest and fastest ways to perform a task.

Warnings and solutions to common problems.

Areas where 1-2-3 release 2.4 differs from release 3.4.

You'll also find sections titled "What's Wrong with This Picture" that provide simple exercises to help you test what you've learned.

Acknowledgments

My thanks go to Seta Frantz, Steve Poland, and the other folks at Alpha Books who helped in making this book a reality.

Dedication

To my wife, Maxine, who—when she saw that I was writing an *Idiot's Guide*—commented, "At least you'll have a big audience."

Trademarks

(The lawyers made me put this stuff in.)

All terms mentioned in this book that are known to be trademarks or service marks are listed below. In addition, terms suspected of being trademarks or service marks have been appropriately capitalized. Alpha Books cannot attest to the accuracy of this information. Use of a term in this book should not be regarded as affecting the validity of any trademark or service mark.

Lotus and 1-2-3 are registered trademarks of Lotus Development Corporation.

SmartIcons is a trademark of Lotus Development Corporation.

Part I
Let's Take It from the Beginning: The Basics of 1-2-3

Lotus 1-2-3 is arguably the most popular computer program in history. This fact leads us to one inescapable conclusion: more people have been puzzled and frustrated by 1-2-3 than by any other program. And since you're looking at this book, I suspect you are one of them. Well, you're in good company!

I've known lots of people who were stumped by 1-2-3, including brain surgeons, mathematicians who can do calculus problems in their heads, and rocket scientists. OK, I made up that last one—I've never known any rocket scientists! But I'll bet that somewhere there's a rocket scientist who was stumped by 1-2-3!

The point here is that learning a computer program has very little to do with being "smart" or "stupid." It's true that a few people seem to take to computers like a duck takes to water. I'm sure you know at least one of these types—they're affectionately called geeks or nerds. But the rest of us have to work at it, and sometimes it can be a difficult and frustrating process that makes you feel like a perfect idiot.

Well, it's not your fault. The problem is not with you, but with the computer program. It's not particularly obvious how to use Lotus 1-2-3, and the program manuals are often confusing and full of computer jargon. You would do a lot better if the material were just presented in a better fashion. And that's where this book comes in.

Chapter 1

The Top Ten Things You Need To Know About Lotus 1-2-3

Most computer books put the summary at the end, but I've decided to put it here at the beginning instead. This way, if you read only this one chapter, you'll learn the most important things about 1-2-3 (though you'll be missing lots of good stuff, so please read the rest of the book!).

1. To start 1-2-3 from the DOS prompt, type **123** and press **Enter**. (See Chapter 2 for more information on the DOS prompt and starting 1-2-3.)

2. To display the main 1-2-3 menu, press /. You use menus to tell 1-2-3 what to do. Without menus, 1-2-3 is about as useful as a fish on rollerskates.

3. To select a command from a menu, press the first character (letter or number) of the command. This method is quicker than the alternative of using the left and right arrow keys to highlight the desired command, then pressing Enter.

4. To cancel a menu command, press **Esc** one or more times. We all make mistakes, and it's nice to be able to get out of them. If you goof while entering a menu command, press **Esc** one or more times to "back out" until the mode indicator reads **READY**.

5. The mode indicator in the top right corner of the screen tells you the current status, or mode, of 1-2-3. The most important modes are:

☛ READY: 1-2-3 is ready for you to enter data or to select a command from the menu.

☛ MENU: The menu is active, and you are entering a menu command.

☛ ERROR: Something is wrong—an error has occurred.

6. To move to the upper left corner of your worksheet, press **Home**. To move to the lower right corner of your worksheet, press **End** and then press **Home**.

7. To move to the end of a row or column of data, press **End** and then press an **arrow** key. For example, to move to the bottom of a column, press **End** followed by ↓.

8. To save your worksheet in a disk file, press / to display the menu, then select File followed by **Save**. You must save your work in a disk file if you want it to be available the next time you use 1-2-3.

9. To use a worksheet that you saved earlier, press / to display the menu, then select File followed by **Retrieve**. Next, use the ← and → arrow keys to highlight the desired worksheet file name, then press **Enter**. When you retrieve a worksheet, it appears exactly as it was the last time you saved it.

10. If you accidentally erase some valuable data (or make some other mistake), press **Alt+F4** to undo it. (This works only if 1-2-3's Undo feature is turned on; see Chapter 4 for details.)

Gee, is that ten already? Well, I can't leave this one out!

11. To quit 1-2-3, press / to display the menu, then select **Quit** followed by Yes. You must quit 1-2-3 in order to use another program; you must also quit before turning your computer off.

Chapter 2
So What Is This Lotus 1-2-3 and How Do I Start It?

In This Chapter

- ☛ What is Lotus 1-2-3?
- ☛ What's it good for?
- ☛ Things you can and cannot do with 1-2-3
- ☛ How to start 1-2-3
- ☛ How to quit 1-2-3

Why Are You Reading This Book?

Since you are reading this book, you probably fall into one of these three categories:

- ☛ You have a computer program called "Lotus 1-2-3" and you are supposed to learn how to use it. You don't have a clue as to what it is, what it's good for, or whether it's low in cholesterol.

☞ You have tried to use Lotus 1-2-3 and are frustrated because you can't get it to do what you want. You're just about ready to take a sledgehammer to your computer.

☞ You thought you were buying a cookbook and are wondering where the "desserts" chapter is.

If it's desserts you're after, I can't help! But if it's 1-2-3 that you're dealing with, 1-2-3 that you're worrying about, 1-2-3 that makes you feel like an idiot, then you've come to the right place. You can relax and take that worried look off your face, because this book is going to solve all your problems. (Well, not ALL your problems—for that you'll need Dear Abby!) But it will teach you—quickly and almost painlessly—how to use Lotus 1-2-3, even though you're not a computer nerd.

So make yourself comfortable and we'll get started. If you're sitting at your computer, that's fine, because you'll be able to try things out right away. If you're not at your computer, that's okay too. You can read now and try stuff out later.

We'll start at the beginning. In this chapter you'll learn what Lotus 1-2-3 is and about some of the things you can use it for. You'll also learn how to start Lotus 1-2-3, and then how to quit the program.

What Is Lotus 1-2-3 and Why Does It Have Such a Silly Name?

1-2-3 is a computer program that helps you work with numbers. In technical "computerese" jargon it's called a *spreadsheet* program, but that's not important (in fact, you can forget it right now if you like!). What is important is what 1-2-3 can do for you. By way of demonstration, let's take a look at the way you might deal with some numbers—your monthly personal budget, for example—without a computer. You might get a piece of paper with rows and columns on it, and total up the last two months' expenses like this:

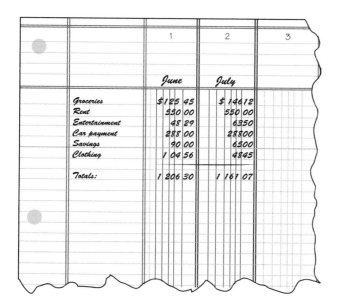

	1	2	3
	June	*July*	
Groceries	$125 45	$ 146 12	
Rent	550 00	550 00	
Entertainment	48 29	63 50	
Car payment	288 00	288 00	
Savings	90 00	65 00	
Clothing	1 04 56	48 45	
Totals:	1 206 30	1 161 07	

Lotus 1-2-3 is designed for working with numbers, such as this personal budget.

As to how Lotus 1-2-3 got its name, here's the scoop. "Lotus" is simply the company name, and the "1-2-3" reflects the fact that the program integrates what the developers believe to be the three most important tools for businesses (more about them later):

1. An electronic *spreadsheet* program for manipulating numbers.
2. *Graphics* for visual display of data.
3. *Database management* for managing lists of information.

Do You Really Need 1-2-3?

Budgets and the like are just the sorts of things that 1-2-3 is designed to do. But you say you don't need a computer for your personal budget? Few people do, unless they happen to be Ross Perot! Imagine, however, that you are working on the annual budget for your entire department, keeping payroll records for 500 employees, or (worse yet!) trying to make sense of your boss' expense account. I think you get my drift—there are some jobs that really need a computer. If you need to work with numbers, you can't do better than Lotus 1-2-3. And while numbers are 1-2-3's main strength, the program is not limited to working with numbers—it can handle words and other text as well.

Things You Can Do with 1-2-3

☞ Keep track of expenses.

☞ Do a profit-and-loss statement.

☞ Create a sales forecast.

☞ Analyze investment performance.

☞ Maintain a mailing list.

Things You Can't Do with 1-2-3

☞ Write a novel.

☞ Play music.

☞ Blast alien spaceships.

☞ Send a fax.

☞ Find Jimmy Hoffa.

Once you learn how to use it, you'll find that 1-2-3 is faster, more accurate, and less prone to mistakes than the old paper-and-pencil method. And if you do make mistakes, it's a lot easier to fix them with 1-2-3. It also lets you do some things you just can't do the old way. Trust me, I know—because I, too, was once a total beginner, and 1-2-3 made me feel like a first-class idiot. And because I didn't have a book like this to help me, it took me ages to learn how to use the program. Now, I use it almost every day and can't imagine getting along without it. I think you'll feel the same way once you get the hang of it.

How Do I Start This Dag-Nabbed Program?

Before you can use the 1-2-3 program to do anything, you must start it. Sometimes starting a program is called "opening" or "running" a program, but knowing this doesn't help much (now there are *three* terms you don't understand instead of only one!). Let's look at an analogous situation.

Think of 1-2-3 as a Videotape

Imagine that you have a library of videotapes. Being a cultured, intellectual type, you decide to watch "Godzilla Eats Wisconsin." The first step is to turn on your VCR and television. But that's not enough, of course. You must also select the tape, put it in the VCR, and push the "Play" button. Now you can grab your popcorn, sit down, and put your feet up.

Computers work in a similar manner. Turning on your computer and monitor is like turning on the TV and VCR—it's necessary, but not enough. You must also tell the computer what program to run—sort of like picking a tape and pushing "Start." And that's what you'll learn next.

Starting 1-2-3 on Your System

The steps that are needed to start 1-2-3 depend on how your computer is set up. Unfortunately, I can't look over your shoulder to see just what your setup is. I can, however, tell you that almost all computers are set up in one of two ways. Yours is probably among them, so one of the following methods should work.

Your Computer Must Be ON First (No Kidding!)

When you turn your computer on, it will whir and click for a minute or two and then settle down. When it does, take a look at the screen. If you're lucky you'll see some sort of list, or menu, displayed. This menu lets you select from the various programs that are installed on the computer. Right now you are looking for the entry for Lotus 1-2-3. It may say "Lotus," or "1-2-3," or "Lotus 1-2-3." If you find it, simply type the letter or number that is displayed next to the entry. That's it! You have just started 1-2-3. Your screen should now look like the figure below, and you can skip ahead to the next section (titled "Now What?").

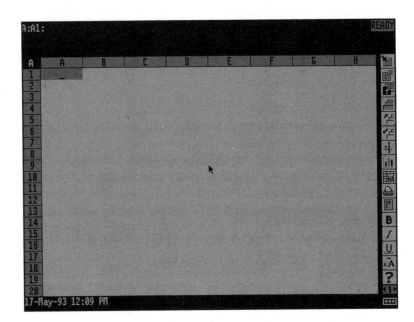

The Lotus 1-2-3 screen.

What, No Menu?

What if you don't see a list when your computer starts? Instead, you'll see a mostly blank screen with something like this displayed:

C:\>

This is called the *DOS prompt*. Don't panic! The DOS prompt is just the computer's way of saying, "Tell me what you want." And that's just what you're going to do.

DOS prompt: An on-screen prompt indicating that your computer is ready to accept a command. It usually looks something like C:\> or C:> (depending on your setup).

The DOS prompt (DOS rhymes with "moss") is responsible for a lot of puzzlement and frustration among computer users. It was invented by evil computer nerds who wanted to ensure that they would always have a job. DOS stands for *Disk Operating System*, which your computer needs to run programs like 1-2-3 and to coordinate its various parts (keyboard, printer, etc.). Just remember: when you see the DOS prompt, it is the computer saying, "What is your command, Master?"

Now, if you ask the computer for an ice cream sundae or a new Ferrari, you're not going to get it! But if you ask it to start Lotus 1-2-3, you will—at least, you will if you ask the right way. There's no need to be polite, but you do need to be precise.

So, how is it done? For starters, try typing in

123

Try typing in **cd \123r24** instead.

and then pressing **Enter**. If you're lucky, this will work; the program will start, and you can go on to the "Now What?" section of this chapter. If it doesn't work, and you see the message "Bad command or file name," don't worry. It just means your computer is not sure where 1-2-3 is installed, and you need to find it. Try typing in

cd \123r34

and then pressing **Enter**.

If the computer answers "Invalid Directory," don't worry. Check your spelling; if you made an error, try again. If it still doesn't work, you can also try typing in

cd \123

or

cd\lotus

(remember to press **Enter** at the end of each line). One of these commands will almost surely work, and your DOS prompt will probably change to

C:\123r34>

or

C:\123>

or

C:\lotus>

You've just completed the first step—sort of like inserting the correct videotape into your VCR. The next step ("pushing Start") is even easier. Type

123

and press **Enter**. The program will start, and the screen should look like the figure below. Congratulations! You are on your way. You can now skip ahead to the "Now What?" section.

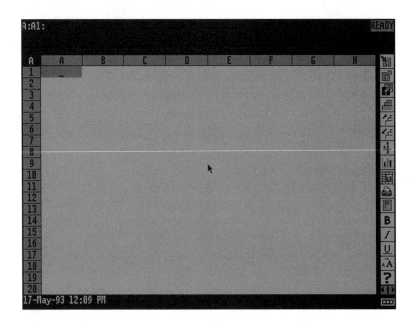

The Lotus 1-2-3 screen.

What If It Doesn't Work?

What if none of this works for you? First, you can mutter a few nasty things about whoever set up your computer, because they definitely did so in a non-standard way. Second, it means you are going to have to call on one of those computer types to help you out (I told you we kept them around for a reason!). Tell them you can't seem to get Lotus 1-2-3 started; they should have things working pretty soon. You should watch what they do, and be sure you understand the steps needed to start 1-2-3 (if your memory is like mine, you'll want to write these down!).

Now What?

Well, you have managed to start 1-2-3. This may not seem like much, but it's an essential step—one that has baffled some people for hours! Now what? Well, you could pat yourself on the back and go get a cup of coffee if you like. Or you could go on to the next chapter and start learning how to use 1-2-3. But maybe you're very busy and there's something important you need to do now (such as lunch!). You'll need to quit 1-2-3; that's the next (and last) topic of this chapter.

Quitting 1-2-3

Quitting 1-2-3 is simple. All you do is press /, then press **Q**, then press **Y**. The program will end, and you'll go back to either the DOS prompt or the menu (depending on how your system is set up). You can now head for the coffee machine, use another program, or turn your computer off and head for home!

If you want to be able to start 1-2-3 from any DOS prompt, without having to use the CD command to change directories, you'll need to edit your AUTOEXEC.BAT file and add the Lotus 1-2-3 directory to the PATH statement. You should NOT try this yourself unless you know what you are doing! Find your local computer whiz and ask him or her to help.

The Least You Need to Know

You're really on your way now!

- ☛ Lotus 1-2-3 is a spreadsheet program that is designed to work with numbers.

- ☛ If your computer displays a menu when it is turned on, you start 1-2-3 by selecting "Lotus 1-2-3" or "1-2-3" from the menu.

- ☛ If your computer is not equipped with a menu system, you start 1-2-3 by typing **123** at the DOS prompt.

- ☛ The DOS prompt is that weird C:\ thing on your screen that is the computer's way of saying, "Tell me what to do, Master."

- ☛ To quit 1-2-3 you type **/QY**.

This page unintentionally left blank.

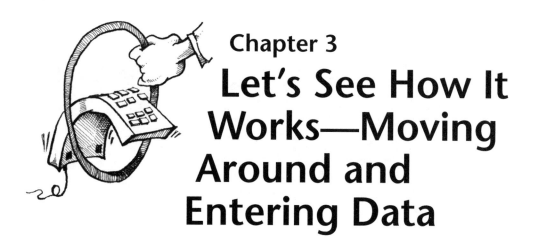

Chapter 3
Let's See How It Works—Moving Around and Entering Data

In This Chapter

- Parts of the 1-2-3 screen
- Cells and cell addresses
- How to move around in 1-2-3
- What kinds of data can you use?
- Entering data into the worksheet
- Editing data

Anatomy of a Screen

When you start Lotus 1-2-3, you'll be looking at the 1-2-3 screen with an empty, or blank, *worksheet*. What now? The screen you see is rather complicated—and since you'll be spending lots of time looking at it, you should know what its parts are.

The figure shows the screen with its most important parts labeled. Don't worry about what these things do for now—you'll learn all about it soon enough. For now, it'll be enough if you remember what things are called so you'll know what I'm talking about!

Current cell address   Control panel   Mode indicator   SmartIcons

Cell pointer

Worksheet

The main parts of the 1-2-3 screen.

Status line

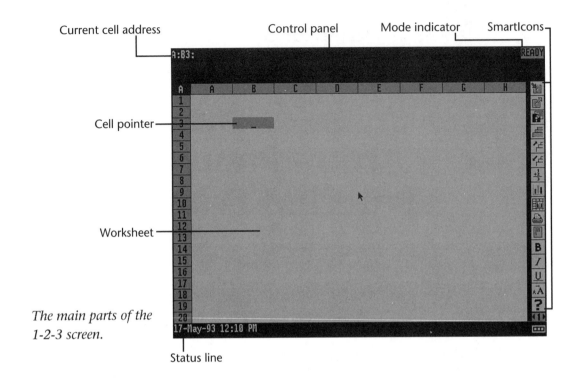

SPEAK LIKE A GEEK

The **worksheet** is the area of the screen where you enter data and perform calculations.

You'll be learning about all these parts of the screen as we go along. In keeping with the spirit of the book, I'll be presenting only the essential information, leaving the unnecessary technical stuff out. For starters, here are brief descriptions.

☛ **Control panel:** used by 1-2-3 to display data, menus, and other items as you work.

☛ **Cell:** a location in the worksheet where you can enter data.

☛ **Cell pointer:** indicates the currently active cell, or location, in the worksheet.

☛ **Current cell address:** indicates the address of the cell containing the cell pointer.

- ☞ **Mode indicator:** indicates the current condition of the program. This normally displays **READY**, indicating that 1-2-3 is ready for you to enter data or a command.

- ☞ **Worksheet:** area of the screen where you enter, edit, and manipulate data.

- ☞ **Status line:** displays the date and time. Also displays indicators if the NumLock, CapsLock, or ScrollLock key is "on."

- ☞ **SmartIcons:** Small pictures that you can click with the mouse to perform certain tasks.

The SmartIcon area of your screen will look slightly different from the figure. Don't worry—this is a minor difference that is not important.

Help! My Screen Doesn't Look Like That!

If your screen looks different from the figure, with no SmartIcons and some other differences, it's OK. There's no need to panic. It means only that your copy of 1-2-3 is operating in a display mode that's different from the one I was using when I made the figure.

You now have two choices. You can turn ahead to Chapter 4 for more details on 1-2-3's display modes, and on how to switch to the "proper" mode, or (and this is my suggestion) you can just continue with this chapter. Everything you'll learn in this chapter applies equally to both of 1-2-3's display modes.

SPEAK LIKE A GEEK

The term **display mode** simply means the way a computer program displays things on the screen. Many programs, including 1-2-3, have two or more display modes.

Cells, Cells, and More Cells

Every 1-2-3 worksheet consists of cells—lots and lots of cells (we'll figure out just how many soon). I'm not talking about jail cells here, or the kind of cells you studied in biology class. In 1-2-3, a *cell* is a storage compartment, a location where you put data, or information, that you are working with.

The cells in a worksheet are organized in *rows* and *columns*. Each column is identified by a letter, and each row is identified by a number. You can see these letters and numbers displayed along the top and left edges of the worksheet. As you've probably figured out already, each cell can be identified by its column and row. And that's exactly how each cell gets an *address*: its column letter followed by its row number. The cell in column A and row 1 has the address A1, and so on.

By the way, you won't see the cells themselves until they have some data in them. This is because 1-2-3 normally does not draw borders around the cells. Trust me, though—the cells are there!

Rows and Columns, Columns and Rows

When you start 1-2-3, you'll see maybe eight columns (A through H) and 20 rows on the screen, for a total of 160 cells. This is only a tiny fraction of the cells that a worksheet contains, however. In fact, a 1-2-3 worksheet contains 8,192 rows and 256 columns! If you whip out your calculator, you can quickly figure out that there are 2,097,152 cells in a worksheet. Gadzooks, that's a lot of cells! What on earth would you ever do with over two million worksheet cells?

The answer is "not much." The truth is that the great majority of worksheets use only a small part of the total capacity. It's nice to have all those cells available if you need them, but usually most of them just sit there empty.

> ### By the Way . . .
> The last time I checked, the alphabet still had only 26 letters—so how are 265 columns identified? The first 26 columns are labeled A through Z; after that, double letters are used. After column Z there's column AA, AB, AC, and so on up to AZ. Column AZ is followed by column BA, BB, BC, and so on up to the 256th column, IV (that's "eye-vee," and not the Roman numeral four!).

You Really Get Around

Lots of the things you will be doing with 1-2-3 involve individual cells. You'll be putting data in cells, erasing data from cells, and more. In all these cases, you need some way to tell 1-2-3 which cell you want to work with. You do this by *pointing* at the cell.

How does one point at a worksheet cell? With the cell pointer, of course! The *cell pointer* is a small rectangle that occupies a single worksheet cell at a time. When you start 1-2-3, the cell pointer is in cell A1, but you can move it to any other cell. Your actions will affect whichever cell the cell pointer is in.

Pointing Here, Pointing There

You can move the cell pointer using either the keyboard or, if your computer has one, the mouse. Some people prefer the keyboard, others favor the little rodent—excuse me, mouse.

> **E·Z**
> To quickly determine the address of the cell pointer, look at the current cell address indicator in the control panel.

By the Way . . .

My opinion—and I think most experienced 1-2-3 users would agree—is that it's faster and more efficient to move the cell pointer with the keyboard. Since your hands must be on the keyboard to enter data, it wastes time and effort to move the mouse whenever you want to move the cell pointer.

By the Way . . .

When you press **End**, 1-2-3 displays the END indicator in the lower right corner of the screen. This is helpful for those of us who often forget what we just did two seconds ago! Press **End** again to cancel and remove the END indicator.

Here's a summary of keys you can press to move the cell pointer:

Press this:	To move the cell pointer:
Any arrow key	One cell in the indicated direction.
PgUp or PgDn	One screen up or down.
Tab or Ctrl+→	One screen right.
Shift+Tab or Ctrl+←	One screen left.
Home	To cell A1.
End, Home	To the worksheet's last row and column containing data.
End, arrow key	In the indicated direction to the first non-empty cell that is next to an empty cell.
F5	To the address you specify.

Mousing Around

It's easy to use the mouse to move the cell pointer to a cell that is visible on the screen. All you do is move the mouse until the mouse pointer is over the cell, then *click* (press and release the left mouse button). Voilà!

Using the mouse to move the cell pointer to a cell that is not visible is a bit more involved. You must use the *scroll icons*, four small triangles pointing in different directions that you click on to move the cell pointer. The scroll icons are shown in the following figure. Point at a scroll icon and click to move the cell pointer in the indicated direction. Point and hold down the mouse button to move more than one cell.

The easiest way to move the cell pointer to a specific cell is the F5, or "go to," key. Press **F5**, and on the second line of the screen, 1-2-3 prompts you "Enter address to go to:." Type in the desired cell address and press **Enter**.

SPEAK LIKE A GEEK

The **mouse pointer** is that little doohickey on the screen that moves when you move your mouse.

Scroll icons

Click on the scroll icons to move the cell pointer.

Click here to switch between SmartIcons and scroll icons.

However, the scroll icons are normally hidden by the SmartIcons. What to do? You can hide the SmartIcons and display the scroll icons by clicking on the small rectangle in the lower right corner of the screen. To get the SmartIcons back, click on the rectangle again.

By the Way . . .

Forget about the scroll icons. If you like to use the mouse it's much handier to have the SmartIcons displayed. Anyway, in my humble opinion, it's easier to move the cell pointer using the keyboard.

Scroll Icons and Version 2.4

Hiding the SmartIcons and displaying the scroll icons is a bit more involved in 1-2-3 version 2.4. This is because the SmartIcons are an *add-in*, and not an integral part of the 1-2-3 program (as they are in version 3.4). You can refer to the 1-2-3 documentation if you want to learn about add-ins, but it's not necessary in order to use the program. For now, if you're bound and determined to get at those scroll icons, follow these steps:

1. Press **Alt+F10** to show the Add-in menu, then press **D** to select the Detach command from the menu.

2. Use the ← and → keys to position the highlight over the word **ICONS** (on the third line of the control panel).

3. Press **Enter**, then press **Q** to quit.

Entering Data (At Last!)

We are finally to the point where you will start entering some actual data into a 1-2-3 worksheet. After all, that's what it's all about, isn't it?

Each and every one of those two-million-plus worksheet cells can hold *data*—some chunk of information you're working with. You'll be thrilled to know that there are two different kinds of data:

☞ A *value* is any sort of number. For example, **25**, **–146**, **3.78**, etc.

☞ A *label* is any text entry that is not a value. For example, **Expenses**, **Income**, **August 6**.

This difference may seem trivial to you, but it's important to 1-2-3. 1-2-3 can do certain things with values—such as use them in calculations and display them on graphs—that it can't do with labels. In addition, labels are normally displayed in the worksheet aligned with the left edge of the cell, while values are aligned with the right edge. Fortunately, 1-2-3 is pretty good at telling whether a particular chunk of data is a value or a label; when it's not sure, you can help it along.

Before entering any data, of course, you must move the cell pointer to the cell where you want the data to appear. Also, be sure that 1-2-3 is in READY mode, as indicated by the mode indicator (what else?). If the mode indicator says anything other than READY, try pressing the **Esc** key once or twice.

Entering a Value

To enter a value, simply start typing it. Since it's a value, the first character will be one of the following:

    0 1 2 3 4 5 6 7 8 9 + – . $

On the basis of the first character you type, 1-2-3 recognizes the entry as a value, and immediately changes the mode indicator to VALUE. 1-2-3 also recognizes the characters (@ and # as the start of a value; you'll understand the relationship of these characters to values when you learn about formulas in Chapter 9.

As you continue to type the value, you may wonder why nothing is appearing in the cell. No, you haven't entered the Twilight Zone! As you type data, it appears not in the cell, but on the second line of the control panel. You'll see the data entry in the worksheet cell only after you confirm the entry, which you do by either pressing **Enter** or by moving the cell pointer to another cell.

When entering a number, use a leading minus sign (–) to indicate a negative number; do not enclose the number in parentheses (as some accountants do for negative numbers). You can include a leading dollar sign ($), but it will be ignored. Do not include commas or spaces.

Entering a Label

Entering a label is not really any different from entering a value. Move the cell pointer to the desired cell and start typing. If the first character is anything other than one of the number characters

0 through 9, as well as + – . $ (@ #

If you make a mistake while entering data, press **Backspace** one or more times to erase the offending characters, then retype the data. To cancel the entire entry, press **Esc**.

then 1-2-3 recognizes the entry as a label, and displays **LABEL** in the mode indicator. The label appears in the control panel as you type, then is entered in the worksheet cell when you confirm the entry by pressing **Enter** or by moving the cell pointer to another cell.

Labels That Look Like Values

Some labels can confuse 1-2-3 because they start with a numeric character. For example, the street address **402 Oak Street** begins with a number, so when you start entering it, 1-2-3 goes into VALUE mode. When you try to confirm the entry, however, 1-2-3 chokes on the non-numeric characters, beeps at you, and enters EDIT mode so you can fix things. See the "Editing Your Data" section (later in the chapter) to learn how to use EDIT mode to fix mistakes such as these.

Label prefix character: One of three special characters (' " and ^) that mark a cell entry as a label, and tell 1-2-3 how to align the label in the cell.

To avoid this problem, type a ' (that's an apostrophe) as the first character of the label. Thus, if you type

'402 Oak Street

you'll be OK. The ' is a label prefix character that tells 1-2-3 the entry is a label even though it starts with a numeric character. You actually have a choice of three label prefix characters.

1-2-3 stores all labels with a *label prefix character*. This character serves two purposes: it specifies that the entry is a label, and it determines how the label is aligned in the cell. There are three label alignment choices: left, right, and center. Each alignment is associated with a particular label prefix character: ' for left, " for right, and ^ for center.

There's a fourth label prefix character, \, that does not affect alignment. Rather, it tells 1-2-3 to repeat the cell entry across the width of the cell. For example, if you enter \- in a cell, it will display a row of dashes across the entire cell.

1-2-3 does not display a label's prefix character in the worksheet. It is, however, displayed in the control panel (along with the rest of the cell's data) when the cell pointer is on the cell. In fact, whenever 1-2-3 is in READY mode, the control panel displays the contents of the cell that the cell pointer is on.

By the Way . . .

Values are always displayed right-aligned. There's nothing you can do about it, so why complain?

Alignment only applies to labels that are narrower than the cell they're in. If the label length exceeds the cell width, it is displayed left-aligned, and one of two things happens:

- ☛ If the cell(s) to the immediate right are empty, the entire label is displayed.

- ☛ If the cell(s) to the immediate right contain data, only part of the label is displayed. The entire label is still in the cell—you just can't see it all. (You'll learn how to change column width in Chapter 7.)

By the Way . . .

A common use of labels is as column headings, to identify columns of numbers in a worksheet. Because values are always right-aligned, the default left-aligned labels don't look good when used as column headings. Your worksheets will be more attractive (and easier to read) if you use right- or center-aligned labels at the top of columns.

What if you enter a date (such as 9/2/93) and 1-2-3 displays a value (such as 32414)? What has happened is that you forgot the label prefix character, so 1-2-3 treats the entry as a date—and converts it automatically to a date serial number (explained next).

How About a Date?

Because lots of worksheet-type tasks involve dates, you'll need to know how to enter them. You have two choices; one method is easy, the other is a bit tricky (but a lot more flexible).

The easy method is simply to enter a date as a label. For "November 8, 1993" you could type in

Nov. 8, 1993

or

'11/8/93

Note the *label prefix character* in the second example, necessary because the first character of the date is a number. Dates entered as labels look fine, and are OK for some situations.

What's Your Serial Number, Mac?

For more flexibility, however, you'll want to make use of 1-2-3's special date features. These features let you perform certain useful date calculations, such as determining the number of days between two dates, and also give you a choice of date display formats.

To enter a date, you use the @DATE function. This is one of 1-2-3's special functions, which are covered in more detail in Chapter 10. For now, let's just worry about how it works. To enter a particular date in a cell—say November 8, 1993—move the cell pointer to the cell and type

   @DATE(93,11,8)

then press **Enter**. (Note that you must provide the function with the year, month, and day information in that specific order). The cell displays **34281**. Help! Surely that's not right!

Date serial number: The number of days between January 1, 1900 and the current date.

   Calm down! It is, in fact, OK. You see, 1-2-3 stores each date as a *serial number* that gives the number of days since the start of the century, January 1, 1900 (which has a serial number of 1). You can get out your old calendars and verify that there are, in fact, 34,281 days between January 1, 1900 and November 8, 1993. Or, you can take 1-2-3's word for it (I thought you would!).

> ## By the Way . . .
>
> To use the @DATE function to enter dates in the next century, use three digit numbers, starting with 100, for the year. For example, January 10, 2000 would be entered as @DATE(100,1,10).

   Now, having a date displayed as a serial number is about as useful as a fish on a bicycle. To display it in a standard date format, you will have to change the cell's display format. You'll learn how in Chapter 12.

The Cell's Already Occupied!

If the cell already has data in it, no problem. The new entry simply replaces the old entry (unless you press **Esc** before confirming the new entry, in which case the original data stays put).

Editing Your Data

What if you want to change data that has already been entered in a cell? No problem. You can simply enter new data in the cell, and it will replace the old data. More often, however, you'll want to edit the existing data, making minor changes such as correcting a misspelling.

The term **default** refers to 1-2-3's standard way of operation. There are many program settings you can change; if you do not change them, 1-2-3 will use the default.

To edit data, move the cell pointer to the cell and press **F2**. 1-2-3 enters EDIT mode, as indicated by the mode indicator. You do not edit directly in the worksheet, but rather in the control panel display.

As you know, the control panel displays the contents of the current cell. While in EDIT mode the control panel also displays a small, blinking *cursor* that indicates where your editing actions will happen. For example, any new character you type appears at the cursor. You can also move the cursor around and delete characters. This table shows you the keys to press.

In EDIT mode, press this:	To do this:
←, →	Move the cursor one character left or right.
Home, End	Move the cursor to the beginning or end of the cell entry.
Tab or Ctrl+→	Move the cursor 5 characters right.
Shift+Tab or Ctrl+←	Move the cursor 5 characters left.
Del	Erase the character at the cursor.
Backspace	Erase the character to the left of the cursor.
Enter	Enter changes in the worksheet, and return to READY mode with the cell pointer in the same cell.
↑ or ↓	Enter changes in the worksheet, and return to READY mode with the cell pointer moved up or down one cell.

The Least You Need to Know

The basics of moving the cell pointer—and of entering and editing data—are not too difficult. Just remember these points:

- ☞ Use the ←, →, ↑, and ↓ keys to move the cell pointer one cell at a time.

- ☞ Use the **PgUp, PgDn, Tab**, and **Shift+Tab** keys to move the cell pointer one screen at a time.

- ☞ To enter data, type it in, and then press **Enter** or move the cell pointer.

- ☞ To enter a label that starts with a number, be sure to enter the label prefix character (' " ^ or \) first.

- ☞ To edit an existing cell entry, move the cell pointer to the cell and press **F2**.

This page unintentionally left blank.

Chapter 4
Modes, Menus, and More

In This Chapter

- ☛ Using 1-2-3's menus
- ☛ The Undo feature
- ☛ Display modes
- ☛ The 1-2-3 Help system

You probably realize by now that when you're using 1-2-3, you are in charge. The program is not going to do one blessed thing unless you tell it to! The problem, of course, is that 1-2-3 is sort of stupid. It only understands one language—its own. That language consists of menus and (in Release 2.4) dialog boxes—and this chapter shows you how to use them.

You'll also learn how to get 1-2-3 to correct your mistakes, how to change the screen display, and how to get program help while you're working.

May I See the Menu, Please?

1-2-3 relies heavily on menus. That's a polite way of saying that without 1-2-3's menus, you're a dead duck. There's very little you can do in 1-2-3 without the menus, so let's see just how they work.

The 1-2-3 menus contain commands that you can select. These commands tell 1-2-3 to *do* all the neat things it is capable of doing. There must be at least a couple of hundred different menu commands in 1-2-3, and while a restaurant menu might be able to handle this many items, a computer program cannot—at least not all at once. How is this handled?

The menu commands are logically organized in a branching structure. (See Appendix A for an outline of the menus.) No more than ten or so menu commands are ever displayed on screen at one time. As you select commands, you work your way down through two or more levels of commands until you reach the final command that actually does something (like print a graph or format some data).

Displaying the Main Menu

To display 1-2-3's main, or top, menu press the / key. You can also display this menu by moving the mouse pointer into the control panel area. The menu will suddenly appear on the second line of the control panel, and the mode indicator will change to MENU. The figure that follows shows the main 1-2-3 menu. Note that the first command on the menu, **Worksheet**, is highlighted.

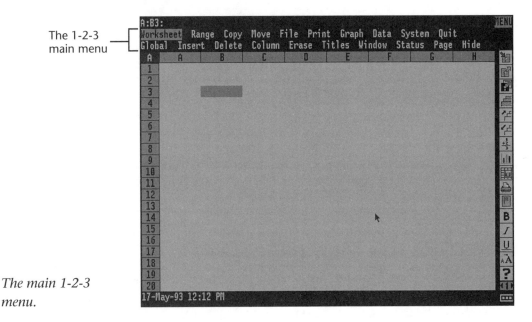

The 1-2-3 main menu

The main 1-2-3 menu.

But what's that on the third line of the control panel, just below the menu commands? It looks like another menu, but it's not. Whenever a menu is displayed on the second line of the control panel, the third line displays a description of whichever command is highlighted on the menu. This description takes one of two forms, depending on the highlighted command:

☛ If selecting the highlighted command leads to another menu level, then the description consists of a list of the commands on that next menu.

☛ If selecting the highlighted command carries out some other action, the description provides a brief explanation of how the command works.

> ## By the Way . . .
>
> If you're having trouble remembering which menu command you need, make use of the command description feature. Display a menu, then use the ← and → keys to move the highlight to different commands. By viewing the descriptions, you may be able to figure out which command you need.

I'm Ready to Order

There are three different ways to make a selection from 1-2-3's menu:

☛ Position the mouse pointer on the command and click the left button.

☛ Type the first letter of the command.

☛ Use the ← and → keys to highlight the command, then press **Enter**.

> ## By the Way . . .
> The third method given above, highlighting the command and pressing **Enter**, is really slow. Don't use it unless you're trying to waste time.

When you select a menu command, one of three things will happen (depending on the command, of course). The next menu is displayed, a dialog box is displayed (Release 2.4 only), or an action is carried out.

You'll notice a difference between the two releases of 1-2-3: release 2.4 uses dialog boxes, and release 3.4 does not. A *dialog box* is something that 1-2-3 uses to get information from you that it needs to carry out the command. Release 3.4 will get the same information—it just uses menu commands rather than dialog boxes to do so. Dialog boxes are covered later in this chapter.

Put It in Reverse, Charlie

If you start entering a series of menu commands and then realize you've made a mistake, it's easy to reverse your actions by pressing the **Esc** key one or more times. Each press of Esc "backs up" one menu level. You can back up all the way until 1-2-3 is in READY mode again, or you can back up part way and then enter other commands to take you down another branch of the menu tree.

Pressing Esc can get you out of the menus, but it cannot undo a command once it has been executed. For that you need the Undo command, discussed soon.

Menu Shorthand

Throughout the rest of this book I'll be telling you to enter lots of menu commands (I'm the bossy type). I'll be using a kind of shorthand—if I say "select /File Save" I mean "press / to display the menu, select File from the main menu, then select Save from the next menu." Got it? Good!

Dialing for Dialog Boxes

Putting a *dialog box* on screen is one method that 1-2-3 uses to exchange information with you. The term "exchange" is appropriate here, because information flows both ways: from 1-2-3 to you and from you to 1-2-3. A major difference between releases 2.4 and 3.4 of 1-2-3 is that 2.4 uses dialog boxes, and 3.4 does not.

Now, this does not mean that release 3.4 is somehow handicapped. It will get all the information from you that it needs, and will also display information you need to be aware of. The only difference is how it's done.

If you're using release 2.4, you'll need to read the rest of this section. Otherwise you can skip it.

Parts of a Dialog Box

1-2-3 displays a dialog box in response to certain commands. A dialog box displays certain information about the program settings and operation, and lets you modify these settings as needed. As you would expect, the information in a particular dialog box is related to the command that displayed the dialog box.

There are dozens of dialog boxes in 1-2-3, each somewhat different from the next. This may seem like an awful lot to learn, but it's really rather simple, because all dialog boxes are made up of the same five elements. These elements are used differently in each dialog box, and not all dialog boxes use all five elements—but once you know how to work with all the elements, you'll be able to handle any dialog box that 1-2-3 throws at you.

Take a look at the dialog box in the figure. This is the Global Settings dialog box. Four of the common dialog box components are illustrated here. We will see what they are and how they work. But first you need to know how to select dialog box items.

Check box ——

Option buttons ——

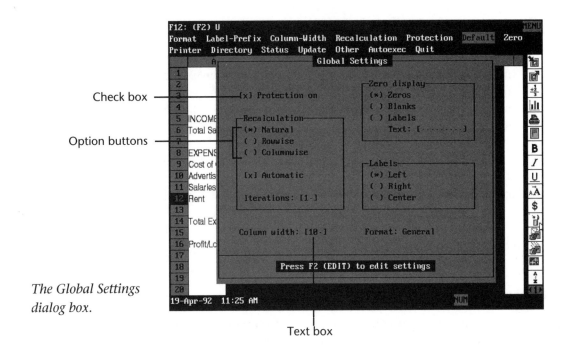

The Global Settings
dialog box.

Text box

When a dialog box is first displayed it is not active—you can view the dialog box settings, but cannot change them. To edit the dialog box, you must first press **F2**.

Your Selection, Please

A dialog box contains many items, but you can modify only one item at a time. You must select the item of interest first. 1-2-3 indicates which dialog box item is selected by highlighting it—or, when the item is already highlighted, by displaying small triangles on either side of the item.

Here's how to select items in a dialog box:

☛ With the mouse, simply point at the item and click.

☛ With the keyboard, press the letter that is highlighted in the item. This is usually, but not always, the first letter.

☛ As an alternate keyboard method, press **Tab** and **Shift+Tab** to move to the next or previous item.

Check Box

A *check box* consists of a descriptive label with a pair of square brackets next to it. A check box is used for a program setting that can be turned on (indicated by an X displayed in the brackets) or off (empty brackets). To switch a check box between on and off, click on it with the mouse, press its highlighted letter, or select it (using **Tab** or **Shift+Tab**) and press **Spacebar**.

Option Button

An *option button* is a label with a pair of parentheses next to it. Option buttons always come in groups of two or more, enclosed in a titled box. Within a group of option buttons, one (and only one) option can be turned on at a time. The "on" option is indicated by an asterisk in the parentheses: (*).

You can turn on an option button by clicking on it with the mouse. With the keyboard, press the letter that is highlighted in the option button group title, then press the letter that is highlighted in the option button.

Text Box

A *text box* is used to enter and edit text information. The current text entry is shown in the square brackets following the text box label. To make changes, select the text box by clicking on it, or by pressing the highlighted letter. 1-2-3 then displays a cursor in the text box, and you can type in the new setting. While a text box is active, you can use the standard editing keys such as **Backspace**, **Del**, ←, and →. When you're finished, press **Enter**.

List Box

You'll occasionally run across a fifth type of dialog box element, a *list box*. As its name implies, a list box presents you with a list of choices. The choices are in alphabetical order. To choose one, click on it with the mouse. To make a choice with the keyboard, activate the list box, use the ↑ and ↓ keys to highlight your choice, then press **Enter**.

Some list boxes contain more choices than can be displayed at once. To *scroll* through the entire list, use the ↑ and ↓ keys, or click on the ↑ and ↓ scroll arrows on the right side of the box.

Command Button

A *command button* is used to tell 1-2-3 to do something. Every dialog box has at least one command button, and most have at least two: an OK button, and a Cancel button.

- ☛ When you select the **OK** command button, it tells 1-2-3 to accept the changes you made in the dialog box, and put them into effect.

- ☛ When you select the **Cancel** command button, it tells 1-2-3 to forget all about the changes you made, and go back to the old settings.

In either case, the dialog box is inactivated, but remains displayed. Press **Esc** one or more times to hide the dialog box and return to READY mode.

Some dialog boxes have other command buttons in addition to the standard OK and Cancel buttons. These extra command buttons typically lead you to another dialog box, called a *pop-up dialog box*. These pop-up dialog boxes are no different from regular dialog boxes—they're used only because there are sometimes too many settings to crowd into a single dialog box. You set options and make changes in the usual manner, and when you select OK or Cancel, you return to the original dialog box.

By the Way . . .
You can always tell when a command button leads to another dialog box because its label has an ellipsis (three periods) at the end, like this...

Let's Do the Undo

OK, everyone who thinks they'll make some mistakes while using 1-2-3, raise your hand. I hope you all raised your hands because you will make mistakes—I guarantee it! But that's OK, because 1-2-3 has a nifty feature that lets you correct your mistakes (or at least most of them).

When a dialog box is displayed, pressing **Esc** has the same effect as selecting **Cancel**.

This feature is called Undo, and it lets you reverse most worksheet changes. But for Undo to work it must first be *enabled* (that's a fancy word for "turn on," as in "would you please enable the light?").

Enabling Undo

Unfortunately there's no way to tell if the Undo feature is enabled. To be sure it's on (or off), you must enter the appropriate command. You can also tell 1-2-3 to save the new setting for future sessions:

1. Select /**Worksheet Global Default Other Undo** (Whew! I told you that menu shorthand would come in handy!).

2. Select **Enable** to turn Undo on, or **Disable** to turn it off.

3. If you want your change to be in effect the next time you use 1-2-3, select **Update**. If you want the change to be in effect only for the current work session, omit this step.

4. Select **Quit**.

Using Undo

If you make a boo-boo and you were smart enough to have enabled Undo, simply press the Undo key combination, **Alt+F4**. 1-2-3 will undo your last changes to the worksheet, such as erasing stuff, moving data from one location to another, and changing formatting. In fact, Undo will reverse all worksheet changes that you made since the last time 1-2-3 was in READY mode.

If Undo is enabled, 1-2-3 displays an UNDO indicator on the status line.

Use Undo carefully. Once you press **Alt+F4**, that's it—you cannot "undo the undo" in version 3.4.

If you press **Alt+F4** a second time in version 2.4, 1-2-3 will undo the undo—in other words, it will return the worksheet to its condition before you pressed **Alt+F4** the first time! You can sit there and press **Alt+F4** as many times as you like, and 1-2-3 will continue to switch between the "old" and "new" versions of the worksheet.

Some Things Can't Be Undone

The Undo feature can handle just about any change to the worksheet itself. Certain things, however, are beyond its abilities. Undo will not reverse

- File operations, such as saving or erasing a file.
- More than one "step" backwards.
- Cell-pointer movement.
- Formula recalculation.
- The bad haircut you got last week at Shaky Eddie's Hair Salon.

Display Delights

You spend a lot of time looking at your computer screen, so it's important that a program present an attractive, clear display. In particular, users seem to like it when the display they see on the screen looks like what they'll get when they print something. After all, lots of the work you do in 1-2-3 will end up being printed, and it's a lot easier to design a worksheet for printing if the screen display accurately reflects the printed output.

Another way of putting it is that you want a program to work in such a way that what you see (on the screen) is what you get (from the printer). Appropriately enough, this capability is called WYSIWYG (pronounced "whizzy-wig"), which stands for (you guessed it) **What You See Is What You Get**. 1-2-3 has WYSIWYG capability, provided by an add-in program called (what else?) WYSIWYG.

An *add-in* is a program that works alongside 1-2-3 to provide additional capabilities. WYSIWYG is one such add-in, and there are more available. You don't need to know about add-ins to use 1-2-3, but if you want more information, please refer to the 1-2-3 documentation. For now, let's just worry about WYSIWYG. You can use 1-2-3 with or without WYSIWYG, and many of the program's basic features will be unaffected. WYSIWYG adds so many great display and formatting capabilities to the program, however, that most users consider it an integral part of 1-2-3, rather than an optional extra. And that's just the approach I'm going to take. The remainder of this book assumes that you are using WYSIWYG.

When 1-2-3 is first installed on a computer, the normal procedure is for things to be set up so that WYSIWYG is automatically loaded (or *attached*) each time 1-2-3 is started. This is the best setup, because WYSIWYG will always be available, and you can forget about it. It's simple to tell if you have the WYSIWYG add-in attached. Press : (colon). If a menu appears in the control panel, WYSIWYG is attached and you're all set. Press **Esc** to hide the menu, and you can go on to the next section.

If no menu appears when you press :, then you need to attach WYSIWYG, and also to tell 1-2-3 to attach it automatically each time the program is run. Here's how to load WYSIWYG:

1. Press **Alt+F10** to display the Add-in menu, then select **Load**.

2. Use the ← and → keys to highlight **WYSIWYG.PLC**, then press **Enter**.

3. Select No-Key, then Select **Quit**.

SPEAK LIKE A GEEK

WYSIWYG: Pronounced "whizzy-wig," an acronym for What You See Is What You Get, describing a computer program in which the display on the screen looks essentially the same as printed output. Also the name of a 1-2-3 add-in program that provides WYSIWYG capabilities.

SPEAK LIKE A GEEK

Add-in: A program that works together with 1-2-3 to provide additional features.

1. Press Alt+F10, then select Attach.

2. Use the ← and → keys to highlight **WYSIWYG.ADN**, then press **Enter**.

3. Select No-Key, then Select **Quit**.

1. Select **/Worksheet Global Default**.

2. Press **F2** to activate the dialog box.

3. Press **A** to select Auto-attach add-ins.

4. Press the number of the first empty text box.

5. Type **WYSIWYG** and press **Enter**.

6. Press **Enter** again, then select **Quit**.

Here's how to tell 1-2-3 to load WYSIWYG automatically:

1. Press **Alt+F10**.

2. Select Settings System Set.

3. Use the ← and → keys to highlight **WYSIWYG.PLC**, then press **Enter**.

4. Select Yes No-key Quit Quit.

Help!

If you need help while using 1-2-3, it is easy to get—not only from this book, but from the program itself. 1-2-3 has a built-in *on-line Help system*. As you're working in 1-2-3, you can call up the Help system and see relevant information displayed right on your screen. Not only is the help on-line, it is *context-sensitive*. This means that the Help system "knows" what you were doing in the program when you activated Help, and displays related information.

On-line: Directly available to you on your computer while you are working.

Getting Help

To get on-line help at any time, press **F1**. The Help screen that is displayed depends on what you were doing at the time:

- If you were in READY mode, Help displays its main index.

- If you were in MENU mode, Help displays information on the commands on the menu that was displayed.

- If you were typing in an @function, Help displays information about that function. (See Chapter 10 for more information on @functions.)

The term **context-sensitive help** describes a Help system that displays information relevant to what you were doing (the *context*) when you requested Help.

- If you were entering a value or label in the worksheet, Help displays information about data entry.

- If an error has occurred (in which case, the mode indicator displays ERROR), Help displays information about the error.

Once the Help system is active, you can move around to view any information you want. Each Help screen contains a number of words or phrases that are highlighted. These are *cross-references* that you use to move around Help; when you select a cross-reference, Help displays information on that topic. Most cross-references refer to specific Help topics, but a few are used to navigate. These are the navigation cross-references:

- **Continue:** Displays additional information on the current topic.

- **Previous:** Displays previous information on the current topic.

- **Help Index:** Displays the main help index.

- **@Function Index:** Displays the @function index.

To select a cross-reference term, click on it with the mouse. You can also use the following keys to navigate through help:

Press this key	*To do this*
→, ←, ↑, ↓	Highlight the next or previous cross-reference term.
Backspace	Display the previous Help screen.
End	Highlight the last cross-reference term on the screen.

Press this key	*To do this*
Home	Highlight the first cross-reference term on the screen.
Enter	Select the highlighted cross-reference term.
F1	Display the first Help screen that you saw when you pressed F1 originally.
Esc	Close Help and return to 1-2-3.

The Least You Need to Know

Knowing how to use the 1-2-3 menus is essential. The Undo feature and on-line help are also important parts of 1-2-3. Here are the most important points to remember:

- ☛ To activate the menus, press / or move the mouse pointer into the control panel.

- ☛ To select a menu command, press the key of its first letter, or click on it with the mouse.

- ☛ You can "back out" of the menus by pressing **Esc** one or more times.

- ☛ If you make a mistake, you can usually undo it by pressing **Alt+F4**. The Undo feature works only if it has been enabled.

- ☛ To view on-line help, press **F1** at any time while working in 1-2-3.

Chapter 5
Save It for Next Time

In This Chapter

- ☞ Saving your worksheet on disk
- ☞ Retrieving a worksheet

We've all heard the old adage "A penny saved is a penny earned," and it's good advice indeed—we all feel better if we have something put away for a rainy day.

There's another adage, and it goes "A worksheet saved is a worksheet that you can use again some other time." Well OK, I admit that it's not quite as catchy as the original, but it's true nonetheless!

Save That Worksheet!

Saving a worksheet is not like saving a drowning person by throwing him or her a life preserver. The effect may be the same, however—particularly if the worksheet contains information that's essential to you or your boss! In a nutshell, you must save a worksheet if you want to be able to use it again in the future.

Why Should I Save My Worksheet?

When you create a worksheet and start adding data, all that information is kept in your computer's electronic memory. That's all fine and well, but there's one problem—when the computer is turned off, that memory forgets everything it ever knew. It goes completely blank, and anything that was stored there is, as they say, history.

TECHNO NERD TEACHES

A computer's main memory is called *random access memory*, or *RAM* for short. This name refers to the fact that the computer can get at (or *access*) anything in memory quickly and easily. When you're using a program such as 1-2-3, the program and its data are kept in RAM.

SPEAK LIKE A GEEK

File: A place on a disk where information, such as a worksheet, is stored.

Why not just leave the computer running all the time? That's not really practical—and besides, you can't be sure that there won't be an unexpected power interruption.

Fortunately, all computers have a form of permanent storage called *disk storage*. There are different kinds of disks; some, which can be removed from the computer, are called *floppy disks* or *diskettes*. Others that are not removable are called *hard disks*, *fixed disks*, or *Winchesters*. These details don't matter, however—the important thing is that disks provide a permanent storage location that is not dependent on the computer being turned on.

Most importantly, information stored on a disk can be *retrieved*, or read back off the disk. When you have saved a worksheet, you can retrieve it back into 1-2-3 at some future time, a day, a month, or a year later. You'll be right back where you were when you last saved it, and you can continue working right where you left off.

How to Save a Worksheet for the First Time

When you first start working on a new worksheet, it does not yet have a name. When you save it, therefore, you must assign it a name. To do so, select /File Save. 1-2-3 will display the following prompt:

Enter name of file to save: C:\123R34\FILE0001.WK3

Depending on the specifics of your system, it may say FILE0002.WK3 or some other number, but the idea is the same. 1-2-3 is suggesting that the worksheet be saved on disk C:, in the directory named 123R34, in a file named FILE0001.WK3. However, that's not a very good name for a file, so you'll want to type in your own file name. As soon as you start typing, the FILE0001.WK3 part of the prompt vanishes and is replaced by what you're typing. The name can be up to eight characters long (please see the next section for more information on file names); don't worry about the period or the WK3 part, as 1-2-3 will add those automatically. Press **Enter** and the file will be saved, and you return to READY mode.

What's in a Name?

When you assign a name to a worksheet, it's a real good idea to use a name that will help you identify what's in the worksheet. So, if the worksheet contains the 1993 sales figures for the eastern region you might name the file

Eastern Region Sales 1993

Great idea, but it won't fly. Why not? The geniuses who designed your computer decided that eight characters were all we needed for file names. You are therefore faced with the task of coming up with descriptive names that are eight (or fewer) characters long. It's not

When you select /**File Save**, release 2.4 does not suggest a default file name. Instead the prompt reads

Enter name of file to save: C:\123R24*.WK1

You do the same thing, however—just type in a one-to-eight-character file name and press **Enter**.

TECHNO NERD TEACHES

Each of your computer's disks is identified by a letter followed by a colon. On most computers the main disk is C:. The storage space on each disk is usually divided into a number of *directories*. Lotus 1-2-3 is usually stored in the directory named 123R34. If you want to learn more about disks and directories (and lots of other useful computer-related things), I suggest you get a copy of *The Complete Idiot's Guide to DOS* by Jennifer Flynn.

TECHNO NERD TEACHES

Technically speaking, a file name consists of two parts: the name itself (which can be from one to eight characters long), and a one- to three-character *extension*. A period separates the name and extension. The extension is optional and can be left off, but most programs use the extension to identify the file type. For example, 1-2-3 worksheet files have the WK3 extension (WK1 for release 2.4).

E-Z

When you specify a filename for a worksheet, you do not have to type in the .WK3 part; 1-2-3 will add that automatically.

always easy, but it can be done. For example, for the above worksheet you might use the name

SLS_E_93

(**SALES EASTERN 1993**—get it?)

and for your personal budget

PERSBUDG

(I'll let you figure this one out!)

You'll need to be creative, but it can be done! In addition to the eight-character limit, there are some other rules to follow for worksheet names:

☞ The name can contain letters, numbers, and the _ (underscore) character.

☞ The first character of the name must be a letter.

☞ Strictly speaking, you can also use the characters ! @ # $ ¢ % ^ & ( ) in a file name, as long as they're not the first character. But don't even think about using * or ?.

By the Way . . .

If you want to be really clever and confuse your co-workers, use cryptic file names such as X5RF_01 and ZZ9FOG. But beware—the person who will end up most confused is you!

By the Way . . .

You can have 1-2-3 display the name of the current worksheet file on the *status line* instead of the time. Here's how:

1. Select **/W**orksheet **G**lobal **D**efault **O**ther **C**lock **F**ilename.

2. To have the file name displayed in future work sessions, select **U**pdate. Otherwise, skip this step.

3. Select **Q**uit.

Saving a File That Has Already Been Named

To save a worksheet that has already been named, simply select **/F**ile **S**ave, then press **Enter**. 1-2-3 then displays a menu with three choices on it. These choices relate to the copy of the worksheet that already exists on disk (since the worksheet has a name, you must have already saved it at least once, right?).

Mouse users can quickly save the worksheet by clicking on the **File Save SmartIcon** (the disk with the arrow pointing toward

- ☛ **Cancel:** Return to READY mode without saving the file.

- ☛ **Replace:** Replace the worksheet on disk with the current version.

- ☛ **Backup:** Save the current worksheet after making a backup copy of the existing worksheet file. The backup has the same name, but has a BAK extension instead of WK3.

By the Way . . .

You should memorize the sequence of commands needed to save a file: **/F S Enter R** (or, if you want to keep backups, **/F S Enter B**). You'll be using it a lot!

When Should I Save My Worksheet?

You should certainly save your worksheet before exiting 1-2-3. If you forget to do so and try to exit without saving, 1-2-3 will display a warning message. Because of the warning, it's difficult to exit the program without first saving the worksheet, but a persistent person can do it! Be warned, though, that this is a bad idea. If you exit without saving, then you will lose all changes you made to the worksheet since you last saved it—or, if you have never saved it, you'll lose the entire worksheet!

Put It to Work

Even the most creative person can't always come up with good, descriptive worksheet names. It's a good idea to include a brief description of the worksheet's contents in the worksheet itself. If you place the description in cell A1, it will be instantly visible when you retrieve the worksheet.

A Worksheet by Any Other Name . . .

There may be times when you want to rename a worksheet. Even though it already has a perfectly good name, for some reason you want to assign a different name to it. Perhaps you're going to make some major changes in the worksheet. If you rename it, then you'll still have the original version saved under the original name, and the new version saved under the new name.

To rename a worksheet, select /File Save but *don't* press Enter. Type in the new name first, *then* press **Enter**. That's all there is to it!

Unless, of course, there's already a worksheet on disk with the name you entered. When this happens, 1-2-3 displays a menu that offers three choices: Cancel, Replace, Backup. You certainly don't want to replace the worksheet, so select Cancel to return to READY mode. Think up a new

name for the worksheet (one that will not already be in use!), then select /
File Save again. Type in the new name, and press **Enter**.

Relive the Past

If you're like most people, there are parts of your past you would like to
relive (perhaps your first date), and other parts you would just as soon
forget (your first date?)! One part you would *certainly* like to relive is those
old worksheets that you have so carefully saved. To "relive" a worksheet,
you must retrieve it into 1-2-3. When you do, it will appear exactly as it
was when you last saved it.

Retrieving a Worksheet

To retrieve a worksheet, select /File **R**etrieve. In the control panel, 1-2-3
will display a variety of information you can use to select a worksheet to
retrieve. This is shown in the figure.

Previously saved files

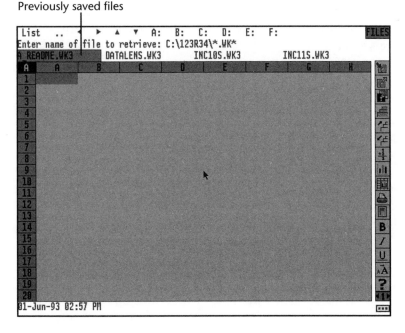

Retrieving a file.

Retrieve: To load a worksheet from disk into 1-2-3
for further editing.

To retrieve a file, mouse
users can click on the **File
Retrieve SmartIcon** (the
diskette with the arrow
pointing out of it).

There are three lines in the control panel. The
first line you can pretty much ignore. The second
line displays the following (or a similar) prompt:

Enter name of file to retrieve: **C:\123R34*.WK***

Let's see what the parts of this prompt mean.
The C: indicates which disk is in use. The 123R34 is
the current directory where worksheet files are
stored. It's OK if your prompt specifies a different
directory. The *.WK* specifies that 1-2-3 should list
all worksheet files that are in the directory.

What if (heaven forbid) you need to retrieve a
file from a different disk or directory? I'll cover that
soon. For now, let's assume that the worksheet file
you want is in the current directory.

The third line of the control panel lists all
worksheet files in the current directory. Here's where you'll select the file
to retrieve. Because this list is only a single line, it can't display all the
worksheet files at once (unless there are only two or three files in the
directory). Here's what to do:

If you already know the
name of the file you want to
retrieve, select /File Retrieve, type in the file name,
then press **Enter**. You don't
have to include the WK3
extension.

- ☞ Press ← or → to move left or right
  in the list, one file at a time.

- ☞ Press **Ctrl+←** or **Ctrl+→** to move
  left or right in the list, four files
  at a time.

- ☞ Press **Home** or **End** to move to the
  beginning or end of the list.

Once the desired file is highlighted, press **Enter**
and the worksheet will be retrieved into 1-2-3.

> ## By the Way . . .
> When you retrieve a worksheet, it replaces the one you're currently working on (if any). If the current worksheet has not been saved, 1-2-3 prompts you to save it before replacing it with the worksheet retrieved from disk.

All Lists Are Not Created Equal

When you select /**File** **R**etrieve, the single-line file list that 1-2-3 presents is not always convenient to work with—particularly if there are lots of worksheet files in the directory. You can get a full-screen file list by pressing **F3** or clicking on **List** on the top line of the control panel. The full-screen list is shown here.

You can retrieve a worksheet when you start 1-2-3 by typing **123**, followed by the worksheet name, at the DOS prompt.

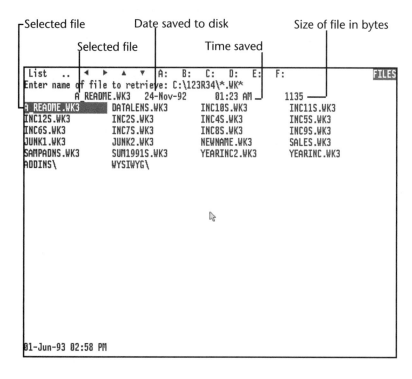

View a full-screen list of worksheet files by pressing F3.

You may see some entries at the end of the file list that end with a backslash, for example ADDINS\. These are not worksheet files, but are *subdirectories* that branch off the current directory. If you accidentally select one of these, press **Esc** twice, then select **Retrieve** again.

The default directory is usually C:\123R24.

Default directory: The directory where 1-2-3 keeps worksheet files (unless you tell it otherwise).

To select a file on this list, highlight it using the ↑, ↓, ←, and → keys, and press **Enter**, or click on the file name with the mouse.

Directory, You're Not My Type

When you select the /File Retrieve command, 1-2-3 automatically looks for worksheet files in the *default directory*. The default directory is also where the /File Save command will save worksheet files. The name and location of the default directory depends on how your system is set up, but usually it is the same place where the 1-2-3 program files are kept: C:\123R34.

The name of the default directory doesn't really matter. What does matter is that there may be times when the file you want to retrieve is not in the default directory, but in some other directory (or even on another disk!). You may also want to save your worksheets in another directory, or on another disk. For example:

- ☞ Your disk might be organized with different directories for different types of worksheets: C:\BUDGETS for your budget worksheets, C:\SALES for your sales worksheets, and so on.

- ☞ You might want to retrieve a worksheet from a floppy disk that a co-worker has given you.

Retrieving a Worksheet from a Different Disk or Directory

You can retrieve a worksheet file from a different directory without changing the default directory. To do this, issue the /File **R**etrieve command. You then change directories (and/or disks) as follows:

- ☛ To move "down" in the directory tree, to a subdirectory of the current directory, highlight the subdirectory name in the file list on the third line of the control panel, then press **Enter**.

- ☛ To move "up" in the directory tree, to the *parent* of the current directory, press **Backspace** or click on the .. in the first line of the control panel.

- ☛ To move to a different disk, click on its letter in the control panel.

If you select a floppy disk drive (usually A: or B:), there are a number of errors that can occur (such as forgetting to insert the diskette, or leaving the disk drive's door open). 1-2-3 will beep and display an error message. You can press **F1** to display Help information related to the error, or press **Esc** to "back up" and continue.

Whenever you use these techniques, you change the directory or disk drive; 1-2-3 lists the new directory's worksheet files and/or subdirectories on the third line of the control panel. If the file you want is listed, highlight its name and press **Enter** to retrieve it. If not, use these techniques to continue looking in other directories.

By the Way . . .

When you retrieve a worksheet file, the /File **S**ave command will always save it back to its original directory, not the default directory.

Changing the Default Directory Temporarily

It's easy to change the default directory on a temporary basis. Select the /File Dir command; 1-2-3 displays the prompt **Enter current directory:** followed by the path of the current default directory. If you start typing, the current directory path will disappear and will be replaced by whatever

you type. Type in the full path, including disk letter, of the new default directory. Finally, press **Enter**.

Use the /File Directory command to change the default directory temporarily.

The new default directory will be in effect immediately, and will be used by both the /File Save and /File Retrieve commands. If you exit 1-2-3 and restart it, however, the original default directory will be in effect again.

Changing the Default Directory Permanently

You can change the default directory more-or-less permanently. By "more-or-less" I mean that the new default directory will be in effect for future 1-2-3 sessions. You can always change it again, of course! Here's how:

1. Select /Worksheet Global Default Dir. 1-2-3 displays the prompt **Default directory:** followed by the path of the current default directory.

2. Press **Backspace** as many times as needed to erase the current entry, then type in the new default directory path.

3. Press **Enter**.

4. Select **Update**, then select **Quit**.

The Least You Need to Know

It's time to see if your brain can "retrieve" any of the information in this chapter. These are the important points:

- ☞ If you want to be able to use a worksheet again, you have to save it to disk with the /File Save command.

- ☞ The first time you save a worksheet you have to assign it a name. Worksheet file names consist of up to eight characters. The extension .WK3 (.WK1 for release 2.4) is automatically added by 1-2-3. Try to assign your worksheets names that will help you to identify their contents.

- ☞ Save your worksheet frequently as you work, particularly before and after you make major changes in it.

- ☞ To retrieve a worksheet that was previously saved, select /File Retrieve, then choose the desired worksheet file from the list displayed.

This page unintentionally left blank.

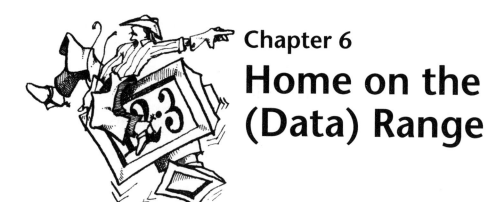

Chapter 6
Home on the (Data) Range

In This Chapter

- ☛ Worksheet ranges
- ☛ Copying and moving data
- ☛ Erasing data

You may not be a cowpoke, but you'll soon feel at "home on the range." This is because something called a *range* is central to many of the things you'll do with 1-2-3. You'll learn what a range is, how to specify one, and how to use ranges to copy, move, and erase worksheet data.

Electric Range or Gas Range?

Neither, actually! In 1-2-3-land, a range is simply a block (or group) of worksheet cells that you have defined. A range can be a single cell, or it can be a rectangular group of two or more cells.

Well, that's simple enough! But what are ranges good for? Actually, they are surprisingly useful, and make many of the tasks you perform in 1-2-3 a whole lot faster and easier. Whenever you define a range, 1-2-3 treats it as a unit. Any command that you enter will affect every cell in the range. So, whenever you want to do something to a group of cells—erase them, for example, or change their formatting—you can define the group of cells as a range and make the desired change with a single command.

Range: A rectangular group of one or more worksheet cells that is treated as a unit.

Range Addresses

The default "range" is the single worksheet cell that contains the cell pointer. You need take no special action to "define" the default range. Generally, however, ranges are at their most useful when they contain more than one cell. Multi-cell ranges can be as big as you like—dozens, hundreds, or thousands of cells. The only restriction is that they must be rectangular. Thus, a range could contain the cells A1, A2, B1, and B2, but the cells A1, B1, C1, and C2 could not make up a range.

A multi-cell range is defined by the cells at its upper left and lower right corners. The address of a range is the two corner cell addresses separated by two periods (..). For example, the range consisting of cells A1, A2, B1, and B2 has the address A1..B2. Three-dimensional ranges are also possible, spanning more than one worksheet. For 3-D ranges, the addresses include the worksheet letters: A:B6..C:D10.

Here's a bit of useless information. A *range address* can consist of the addresses of the cells at any two diagonally-opposite corners—lower right and upper left, for example, or upper right and lower left. 1-2-3 couldn't care less, but the upper-left-to-lower-right address form is standard, and it's probably a good idea to stick to it (for the sake of consistency, if nothing else).

Using Ranges in Commands

There are lots of 1-2-3 commands that operate on ranges; many of them start with /**Range**, but you'll find them scattered in other parts of the menu as well. These commands do different things, but they all work the same way when it comes to specifying the range to operate on.

1. Enter the command (for example, /**Range** Erase).

2. 1-2-3 prompts you to enter a range address. The default range is the address of the current cell, but expressed as a range address. For example, if the cell pointer is on cell B5, the default range address will read B5..B5.

3. If you want the command to affect only the current cell, press **Enter**.

4. To have the command affect a range, type in the range address and press **Enter**.

In step 4, there are two other methods you can use to specify a range: *POINT mode* and a *range name*. These are covered next.

Get the Point?

Human beings, it seems, like to point. That's why we have ten fingers, I guess! Recognizing this fact, 1-2-3 provides a way for you to point at a range rather than specifying its address. You can point with either the keyboard or the mouse.

Unfortunately, 1-2-3 makes things a little bit complicated by providing two slightly different POINT techniques when you're using the keyboard. The difference has to do with anchoring one corner of the range.

Anchors Aweigh

What does an anchor have to do with ranges? Here's how it works. To point at a range, first you'll move the cell pointer to one corner of the range, then use a command to tell 1-2-3, "This is the first corner of the range." This step is called *anchoring*—you are making sure one corner of the range is fixed at a specific location. Then you'll move the cell pointer to the diagonally-opposite corner of the range, and tell 1-2-3, "This is the second corner of the range." (Remember, a range is a rectangle.)

To get back to the differences in anchoring: when you enter certain commands that operate on a range (primarily those that start with /Range), 1-2-3 assumes you have already located the cell pointer at the first corner of the range; the pointer is anchored there automatically. You can go right ahead and move the cell pointer to the other corner of the range. If, however, the cell pointer is not where you want it to be—at one corner of your chosen range—you'll have to unanchor it, move it to the proper cell, and re-anchor it.

With other commands, however, 1-2-3 does *not* assume that the cell pointer is already at the first corner of the range. You must explicitly anchor it before you can point out the range.

So, you're faced with two questions. First, how can you tell when the cell pointer is anchored and when it's not? The answer lies in the range address that 1-2-3 displays after the **Enter range:** prompt. The address will be the address of the current cell (let's say it's cell B5), but it can take two forms:

- ☞ If it's a *range address* (in the form **B5..B5**), then the cell pointer is anchored.

- ☞ If it's a *single cell address* (in the form **B5**), then the cell pointer is not anchored.

The second question is: how do you anchor and unanchor the pointer? That's an easy one! Press the period key (.) to anchor the pointer; press **Esc** to unanchor it.

By the Way . . .

If you use the mouse to point at ranges, then you don't have to worry about anchoring and unanchoring. It's all automatic.

How to Point

Now we can get to the details of how to point at a range.

POINT mode: A worksheet mode that permits you, when entering a command that operates on a range, to "point out" the range by moving the cell pointer.

First, enter the desired command, up to the point where you are prompted for the range. The mode indicator will display **POINT**. Then, with the keyboard:

1. If the cell pointer is already positioned at one corner of the range, press . (period) to anchor it (if it's not already anchored), and go to step 3.

2. Press **Esc** to unanchor the pointer (if it's anchored), move the cell pointer to one corner of the desired range, then press . (period) to anchor the pointer.

3. Move the cell pointer to the diagonally-opposite corner of the range. As you do, a highlighted rectangle appears on the worksheet, showing the current extent of the range. In addition, the **Range:** prompt on the control panel will change to reflect the range address of the highlighted range. This is shown in the figure below.

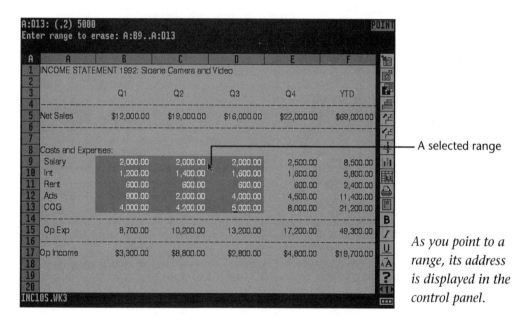

— A selected range

As you point to a range, its address is displayed in the control panel.

4. When the desired range is highlighted, press **Enter.**

By the Way . . .

What if the range you want to highlight extends off the screen? No problem—the worksheet will scroll as needed when you extend the range.

How do you point at a three-dimensional range (Release 3.4 only)? Simply highlight the desired two-dimensional range in the current worksheet (using either the keyboard or the mouse), then press **Ctrl+PgUp** or **Ctrl+PgDn** to extend the range to additional worksheets.

With the mouse:

1. Move the mouse pointer to the cell at one corner of the desired range.

2. Press and hold the left mouse button.

3. Move the mouse pointer to the cell at the opposite corner of the desired range, then release the mouse button. As you move the mouse, a highlighted rectangle is displayed on the worksheet, showing the current extent of the range. In addition, the **Range:** prompt on the control panel will change to reflect the range address of the highlighted range.

4. Press **Enter.**

By the Way . . .

When you are pointing to a range, 1-2-3 displays a blinking cursor in the cell at one corner of the highlighted area. This is the *free cell*, and marks the corner of the highlight that will move in response to the movement keys. You can move the free cell to other corners of the highlight by pressing . (period), allowing you to expand or shrink the range in other directions.

Point First, Ask Questions Later

Free cell: in POINT mode, the cell that marks the movable corner of the highlighted range.

You can specify a range before entering a command. This method—called *preselecting* a range—has an advantage: with most commands, the range will remain selected after the command is executed. This allows you to issue multiple commands that affect the range, without having to specify it more than once.

With the keyboard:

1. Move the cell pointer to one corner of the range.

2. Press **F4**. 1-2-3 displays the current cell address in the control panel, and switches to POINT mode.

3. Move the cell pointer to the opposite corner of the range.

4. Press **Enter**.

With the mouse:

1. Move the mouse pointer to one corner of the range.

2. Press and hold the left mouse button.

3. Move the mouse pointer to the opposite corner of the range.

4. Release the mouse button.

In POINT mode, you can use all of the usual movement keys to expand the range. For example, if the cell pointer is in the upper left corner of a block of data, pressing **End**, → followed by **End**, ↓ will expand the range to cover the entire block.

By the Way . . .

To "unselect" a range, press **Esc**.

Name That Range!

An excellent feature of 1-2-3 is the ability to assign plain English names to worksheet ranges. Once a range has been named, you can use the *range name* anywhere you would otherwise have to specify the range address (for example, in a /**R**ange command or a formula).

Pick a Good Name

It's a good idea to assign a name to a range that describes the information it contains. A range that contains monthly sales figures, for example, might well be called MONTHLY_SALES. You could also name it CHARLIE or X402Y, and 1-2-3 wouldn't know the difference—but you might have some trouble when you look at the worksheet next month and try to figure out what's going on!

There are some rules you must follow when assigning range names (there are always rules, it seems, but that's how computers are!):

- ☞ The name can be up to 15 characters long.

- ☞ The name can contain letters, numbers, and the underscore (_) character.

- ☞ The first character of the name must be a letter.

- ☞ Do not use range names that could be confused with a cell address, such as X10.

You can enter range names using any combination of upper- and lowercase letters—1-2-3 converts everything to uppercase when the name is stored.

Naming a Range

To assign a name to a worksheet range:

1. Select /**Range** Name Create.

2. 1-2-3 displays a list of existing range names, and the **Enter name to create:** prompt. Type in the desired range name, and press **Enter**.

3. The prompt **Enter range:** is displayed. Specify the range by typing in its address, or by using POINT mode.

4. Press **Enter**.

If you want to assign a new range to an existing range name, then in step 2 above, use the ← and → keys to highlight the name of the range, then press **Enter**. 1-2-3 will highlight the range currently assigned to the name. You can use the **arrow** keys to expand or contract the range, or press **Esc** to cancel it entirely then enter a new range.

Deleting a Range Name

If you're no longer using a range name, you may wish to delete it to avoid confusion. Deleting a range name has no effect on the actual worksheet data; it simply deletes the name from the list of named ranges. To delete a range name:

1. Select /**R**ange Name Delete.

2. In the control panel, use the ← and → keys to highlight the name of the range.

3. Press **Enter**.

1-2-3 does not warn you if you delete a range name that is in use, so be careful! You can "undelete" a deleted range name with the Undo command (**Alt+F4**), but only if you use it immediately after the deletion.

Displaying Range Names

Range names are great, but sometimes it's hard to remember them! This is particularly true in a complex worksheet that may have dozens or hundreds of range names. Fortunately, 1-2-3 provides a couple of methods to help you select and keep track of range names.

The first method is useful when you need to enter a range name as part of a command or a formula. Any time that 1-2-3 is prompting you for a range (or when you're entering a formula), you can press **F3** to display all assigned range names on the third line of the control panel. Instead of typing in the range name,

If you delete a range name that is used in worksheet formulas, 1-2-3 replaces all references to the range with its range address. For example, if the name SALES93 was assigned to the range A1..A10, then deleting the range name **SALES93** would result in the formula @SUM(SALES93) being changed to **@SUM(A1..A10)**.

you can use the →, ←, **End**, and **Home** keys to highlight the desired range name, then press **Enter**.

The second method provides a list of all range names and their assigned addresses. You can place this list anywhere in your worksheet for reference:

To delete all range names from your worksheet quickly, select **/R**ange **N**ame **R**eset.

1. Select **/R**ange **N**ames **T**able.

2. In response to the prompt, specify where you want the table to be placed. This location should be an empty region of the worksheet, because the table of range names will over-write any existing data. The table will be two columns wide, and will have one row for each range name.

3. Press **Enter**. 1-2-3 places a list of range names and their assigned ranges in the worksheet, as shown in the figure.

Range name ——

Range address

The /Range Name Table command displays a list of named ranges.

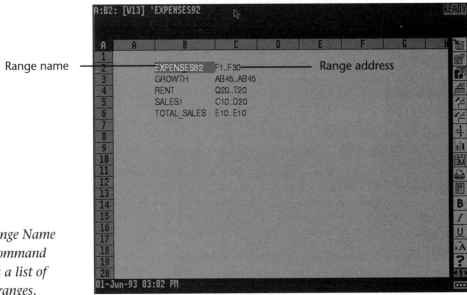

Be a Copy Cat, and Get Moving!

Moving and copying data from one location to another can greatly simplify many worksheet tasks. You can move and copy any type of worksheet data—labels, values, and formulas. The differences between moving and copying are probably obvious, but I'll mention them just to be sure:

☞ When you *copy* data from one location to another, the data exists in both the original and the new locations.

☞ When you *move* data from one location to another, the data is erased from the original location, and exists only in the new location.

When you copy or move data, you work with a FROM range and a TO range. The FROM range is where the data is located originally, and the TO range is where you want the copied or moved data to go.

If you make a mistake copying or moving data, press **Alt+F4** (the Undo key combination) to reverse the operation and restore the worksheet to its initial state. This works only if the Undo feature is enabled (see Chapter 4).

Copying Data

Follow these steps to copy a range of cells to another worksheet location:

1. Select /Copy.

2. 1-2-3 displays the prompt **Enter range to copy FROM:** in the control panel. Specify the FROM range by using POINT mode, or by typing in a range address or range name.

3. 1-2-3 displays the prompt **Enter range to copy TO:**. Specify the TO range by moving the cell pointer to the upper left cell in the range, or by typing the cell's address.

4. Press **Enter**.

That's it! All the data in the FROM range, including any special formatting, will be copied to the TO range.

Moving Data

Moving data from one location to another is very similar to copying data:

1. Select /**Move**.

2. 1-2-3 displays the prompt **Enter range to move FROM:** in the control panel. Specify the FROM range using POINT mode, or by typing in a range address or a range name.

3. 1-2-3 displays the prompt **Enter range to move TO:**. Specify the TO range by moving the cell pointer to the upper left cell in the range, or by typing the cell's address.

4. Press **Enter**.

After a Move operation the FROM range will be blank, and its formatting will be reset to the worksheet defaults.

By the Way . . .

When you copy or move data, any data already present in the TO range is deleted and replaced by the copied or moved data. 1-2-3 gives you no warning of this, so be careful!

Making Multiple Copies

When you're copying data, most of the time you want to make only a single copy. At times, however, you may want to create multiple copies of the data in a single cell. Here's how:

1. Move the cell pointer to the cell whose data you want to make multiple copies of.

2. Select /**Copy**.

3. Press **Enter**.

4. In response to the **Enter range to copy TO:** prompt, specify a TO range that contains the cells that you want the data duplicated in.

5. Press **Enter**. The data in the FROM cell is copied to each and every cell in the TO range.

Erasing Data

To erase the data from a single cell, move the cell pointer to the cell and press **Del**. To erase multiple cells:

1. Select /Range Erase.

2. In response to the prompt, specify the range of cells to erase by using POINT mode, or by entering a range address or range name.

3. Press **Enter**.

To erase a range of cells quickly, preselect the range and press **Del**.

If you delete the wrong cells by mistake, you can get the data back by pressing **Alt+F4** (Undo).

The Least You Need to Know

We have "ranged" far and wide in this chapter, covering all sorts of important information about selecting, naming, and using ranges. Here are the main points:

☞ A range is a block of one or more cells that 1-2-3 treats as a unit. By using ranges, you can have 1-2-3 commands affect multiple cells at once. A range's address consists of the addresses of the cells at the diagonally-opposite corners, separated by two periods (for example, **A1..C5**).

☞ When entering a command, you can specify a range by typing in the range address (or the range name), or by using POINT mode. You can also specify a range before entering a command: drag with the mouse or press **F4**, highlight the range with the **arrow** keys, and then press **Enter**.

continues

continued

☛ To assign a name to a range, select /**R**ange **N**ame **C**reate, enter the name, then specify the range. You can use a range name anywhere 1-2-3 requires a range address.

☛ To copy data from one location to another, use the /**C**opy command. To move data, use /**M**ove.

☛ To erase data from a single cell, move the cell pointer to the cell and press **Del**.

☛ To erase data from a range of cells, use the /**R**ange **E**rase command.

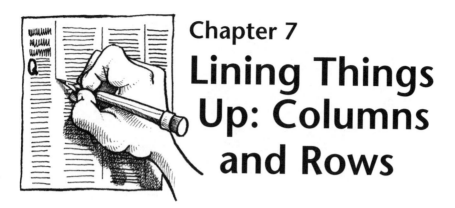

Chapter 7
Lining Things Up: Columns and Rows

In This Chapter

- ☞ Changing the width of columns and the height of rows
- ☞ Adding and deleting rows and columns
- ☞ Hiding columns

The fundamental structure of a worksheet consists of columns and rows. You might think, therefore, that working with columns and rows is an important part of using 1-2-3. You would be absolutely right, of course. Columns and rows may not be the most interesting subject, but you'll find it difficult to create attractive, effective worksheets unless you know how to manipulate them. The figure on the next page shows a worksheet that has used some different column widths and row heights.

If the Column Fits . . .

I have heard it said that a worksheet column can have two possible widths: too wide, and too narrow. That being said, it is still worthwhile to adjust the widths of your columns to best suit the data they contain. If a column is wider than necessary, you waste valuable screen space. If a column is too narrow, one of two things will happen:

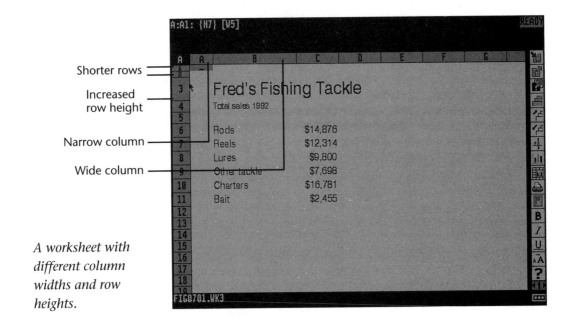

Shorter rows
Increased row height
Narrow column
Wide column

A worksheet with different column widths and row heights.

☞ If a cell contains a *number* that is too wide, the cell displays the number in scientific format, or as a row of asterisks.

☞ If a cell contains a *label* that is too wide, the entire label is displayed if the cell(s) to the immediate right are empty. Otherwise only part of the label is displayed.

Column width is measured in *characters*. That is, a column that has a width of 9 (the default width) will be wide enough to display 9 characters. You can modify the width of worksheet columns to any value between 1 and 240.

By the Way . . .

Column width is measured in terms of characters in 1-2-3's default *font* (the characters used to display data). If you change to a smaller or larger font, then the number of characters that will fit in a column will be more or less, respectively, than the column width.

Changing Column Width

You can change the width of a single column or of a range of adjacent columns. To change the width of a single column:

1. Move the cell pointer to any cell in the column.

2. Select /Worksheet Column Set-Width.

3. In the control panel, 1-2-3 displays the prompt **Enter column width (1..240):**, followed by the current column width. Type in the new column width, or use the ← and → keys to expand or contract the column to the desired width.

4. When your column is the desired width, press **Enter**.

To reset a column to the default width, position the cell pointer in the column and select /**W**orksheet Column **R**eset-Width.

To change the width of two or more adjacent columns:

1. Select /**W**orksheet Column Column-Range Set-Width.

2. 1-2-3 displays the prompt **Enter range for column width change:** in the control panel. Specify the range by using POINT mode, or by typing in a range address. You can specify any range that spans the columns whose width you want to change.

3. Type in the desired column width, or use the ← and → keys to expand or contract the columns to the desired width.

4. Press **Enter**.

Column width: The number of default-size characters that will fit in a column.

If your worksheet displays cells containing rows of asterisks, don't panic! It just means that the column is too narrow to display the number in the cell.

To change a column's width quickly with the mouse, move the mouse pointer into the worksheet frame where the column letters are displayed. Point at the column border (the vertical line to the right of the column letter), press the mouse button, and drag the column to the desired width.

To reset a column to the default width with the mouse, press and hold the **Shift** key, then click on the column border to the right of the column letter.

You can also use the WYSIWYG commands **:Worksheet Column Set-Width** and **:Worksheet Column Reset-Width** to set and reset column widths. These commands work just like their regular 1-2-3 counterparts. Why are there two nearly identical commands that do the same things? Beats me!

To reset two or more adjacent columns to the default width:

1. Select /Worksheet Column Column-Range Reset-Width.

2. 1-2-3 displays the prompt **Enter range of columns to reset:** in the control panel. Specify the range by using POINT mode or by typing in a range address. You can specify any range that spans the columns whose width you want to reset.

3. Press **Enter**.

Changing the Default Column Width

Every column in the worksheet starts out at the default width. This is also the width assigned to any new columns you insert in the worksheet, and to columns whose width you reset. If you feel that most of the information in your worksheet will benefit from a different column width, you can change the default value as follows:

1. Select /Worksheet Global Col-Width.

2. Type in the desired default column width value, or use the ← and → keys to adjust the column width.

3. Press **Enter**.

The new default column width will be applied to all columns, except for those whose width you have changed individually by using the /Worksheet Column Set-width command.

How High Is That Row?

The height of individual rows will also affect the appearance and readability of your worksheet. Changes in row height are most often needed when you use different size fonts in a worksheet. By default, 1-2-3 and WYSIWYG adjust the height of individual rows automatically to match the largest font in that row. In many cases this automatic adjustment is all that is needed, and you don't have to worry about adjusting row height manually. (You can do so, however, if special circumstances call for it.)

Point: A unit of measure used for fonts and for row heights. One point equals 1/72 of an inch.

Row height is measured in terms of *points*. This is the same measure that is used for font sizes, with one point equal to 1/72 of an inch. The automatic row height set by 1-2-3 is normally one or two points larger than the row's largest font. The default font is 12 points, and the default row height is 14 points.

By the Way . . .

1-2-3 will increase a row's height to fit a larger font, but it will not decrease a row's height to fit fonts smaller than the default size. For example, if a row contains nothing larger than 8-point fonts, the automatic row height will remain at the default setting of 14 points.

Changing Row Height

You can change the height of rows manually to any value between 1 and 255 points. When a row is higher than the fonts it contains, text is displayed at the bottom of the row with empty space above it. This can be useful for formatting the worksheet, if you want to include blank space without inserting empty rows. If a row contains a font that is larger than the row's height, the top part of the text is clipped off.

To change the height of one or more rows manually:

1. Select :**W**orksheet **R**ow **S**et-Height.

2. In the control panel, 1-2-3 prompts you for the range of rows to set. Specify a range that includes at least one cell in each row:

either type in a range address, or use POINT mode. Then press **Enter**.

3. Type in the height value, in points, or use the ↑ and ↓ keys to adjust the row(s) to the desired height.

4. Press **Enter**.

By the Way . . .

Don't spend too much time changing row heights unless your worksheet really needs it. The automatic row-height settings are fine for most purposes.

Using Automatic Row Height Adjustment

Automatic row height adjustment is the default, and will be in effect for all rows whose height you have not adjusted manually. If you have made manual changes in the height of one or more rows in your worksheet, you can return them to the default automatic height adjustment by following these steps:

1. Select :Worksheet Row Auto.

2. In the control panel, 1-2-3 prompts you for the range of rows to return to auto height adjustment. Specify a range that includes at least one cell in each row, by either typing in a range address or using POINT mode.

3. Press **Enter**.

Making the Worksheet Fit

As you develop a worksheet, you will often find that you need to reorganize things. You may not have left enough room for some data that you need to insert, or there may be entire rows or columns of data that you want to delete. Sometimes you can use the /Move, /Copy, and /Range Erase commands to do what's needed. Other times, however, it's better to insert or delete entire rows or columns.

Adding More Columns and Rows

You can add one or more new columns or rows anywhere in the worksheet. When you do so, existing data is moved to make room for the new rows or columns. For example, if you insert a new column B, the data that was originally in column B will now be in column C, the data originally in column C will now be in column D, and so on. Likewise with new rows, existing data below the new row is moved down to make room.

> ## By the Way . . .
> Remember that new columns and rows extend the full length or width of the worksheet; they don't just affect the part of the worksheet that's visible on the screen.

To insert one or more new columns:

1. Position the cell pointer in the column where you want the new column(s) placed. For example, to insert a new column between columns A and B, place the cell pointer in column **B**.

2. Select /Worksheet Insert Column.

3. In the control panel, 1-2-3 prompts you for the *column insert range*. To insert a single column, press **Enter**. To insert multiple columns, press → to expand the highlight to the desired number of columns, then press **Enter**.

To insert one or more new rows:

1. Position the cell pointer in the row where you want the new row(s) placed. For example, to insert a new row between rows 5 and 6, place the cell pointer in row **6**.

2. Select /Worksheet Insert Row.

3. In the control panel, 1-2-3 prompts you for the *row insert range*. To insert a single row, press **Enter**. To insert multiple rows, press ↓ to expand the highlight to the desired number of rows, then press **Enter**.

Deleting Columns and Rows

Want to get rid of some rows or columns? No problem! You can delete rows or columns whether they are empty or contain data. In the latter case, of course, the data is deleted as well. When you delete one or more columns, data to the right "moves over" to fill in. For example, if you delete columns B and C, the data that was originally in column D will now be in column B, column E's data will be in column C, and so on. The same is true when you delete rows: existing data moves up to fill in.

To delete one or more columns:

1. Move the cell pointer to the first column to delete.

2. Select /Worksheet **Delete Column**.

3. To delete a single column, press **Enter**. To delete more than one column, press → to expand the highlight to span the desired number of columns, then press **Enter**.

To delete one or more rows:

1. Move the cell pointer to the first row to delete.

2. Select /Worksheet **Delete Row**.

3. To delete a single row, press **Enter**. To delete more than one row, press ↓ to expand the highlight to span the desired number of rows, then press **Enter**.

Use caution when deleting rows and columns. Remember that the entire row or column will be deleted, not just the part visible on your screen. It's all too easy (I know from experience!) to delete something important accidentally, just because it's not visible at the moment. You can recover from a row or column deletion with the Undo command, but only if you issue it *immediately* after the deletion (and, of course, only if Undo is enabled!)

Do You Have Something to Hide?

1-2-3 has the ability to hide one or more columns. Hidden columns do not display on the screen, nor do they appear on printouts. The data in hidden columns is not affected, and remains available for use in formulas and graphs.

Now why on earth would you want to hide worksheet columns? One reason is to hide sensitive information, such as salaries, from prying eyes. You may need that information in the worksheet, but don't want it to appear on the screen or in printed reports. Hiding the columns the data is in will solve the problem.

Here's how to hide one or more columns:

1. Select /Worksheet Column Hide.

2. Move the cell pointer to any cell in the first column you want hidden.

3. To hide a single column, press **Enter**. To hide multiple columns, press . to anchor the range, press → to expand the highlight to span the columns, then press **Enter**.

When you are specifying a range or formula and you enter POINT mode, 1-2-3 displays all hidden columns automatically—with an asterisk next to the column letter to indicate they are hidden. This feature allows you to use POINT mode to include the cells in hidden columns in your formulas and other range commands. When you exit POINT mode, the columns are re-hidden.

Missing some important worksheet data? Check to see if the data is not simply tucked away in hidden columns.

You can re-display hidden columns, removing the "hidden" designation from them and returning them to normal. Here's how:

1. Select /Worksheet Column Display. 1-2-3 displays all hidden columns with an asterisk next to the column letter.

2. Move the cell pointer to the first column to display.

3. To display a single column, press **Enter**. To display multiple columns, press . to anchor the range, press → to expand the highlight to span all the columns you want to display, then press **Enter**.

By the Way . . .

There's no way to hide rows in the same way you can hide columns. You can obtain a similar effect, however, by setting the row height to 1 point. The row will display as a thin horizontal line, but the data it contains will not be visible.

The Least You Need to Know

After reading this chapter, you should have a new-found feeling of power. You now know how to alter a worksheet's basic structure, its columns and rows! Before you get carried away, be sure you remember these points:

- ☛ Column widths are expressed in terms of characters, with the default width being 9. You can change the width of a single column with the /Worksheet Column Set-Width command, or of multiple columns with the /Worksheet Column Column-range Set-width command.

- ☛ Row height is expressed in terms of points, with 1 point equal to 1/72 of an inch. Row heights are normally set automatically to fit the font sizes in the row. You can set row height manually with the :Worksheet Row Set-height command.

- ☛ To add new, empty columns or rows to a worksheet, use the /Worksheet Insert Column or /Worksheet Insert Row command. To delete entire columns or rows and their data, use /Worksheet Delete Column or /Worksheet Delete Row.

- ☛ You can hide one or more columns from view and prevent them from appearing on printouts with the /Worksheet Column Hide command. To display hidden columns, use /Worksheet Column Display.

Chapter 8

Using the Third Dimension (and Living to Tell About It)

In This Chapter

- ☞ Using three-dimensional worksheets
- ☞ Adding and deleting sheets
- ☞ Moving around in the third dimension
- ☞ Using Group mode

You may think that 1-2-3 is complicated enough without dragging in the third dimension. It sounds more like late-night television than a computer program! But the ability to use the third dimension is one of 1-2-3's most powerful features. You may never use it, but if you do, I think you'll agree that you wouldn't want to live without it!

What Is the Third Dimension?

The *third dimension* is not some weird science fiction story! Rather, it is a powerful feature of 1-2-3 release 3.4 that provides you with a great deal of additional flexibility in worksheet design. But what exactly is the third dimension?

If you're using release 2.4, you can skip this chapter. Release 2.4 does not support Three-D worksheets.

Think back to the analogy that compares a worksheet with a sheet of accountant's ledger paper that is ruled into rows and columns. The columns are one dimension, and the rows are the second dimension. Thus, a single sheet of ledger paper can be considered two-dimensional.

Now think of a book containing many sheets of ledger paper. Each sheet still has its two dimensions, but now there's a third dimension—the multiple pages. A particular entry in the book is identified by three items: its row, its column, and its page.

A three-dimensional worksheet file is very similar. It contains multiple worksheets, each of which is like a single page in the ledger book. A cell in the three-dimensional worksheet file is identified by its row, column, *and* worksheet. The structure of a three-dimensional worksheet file is illustrated here.

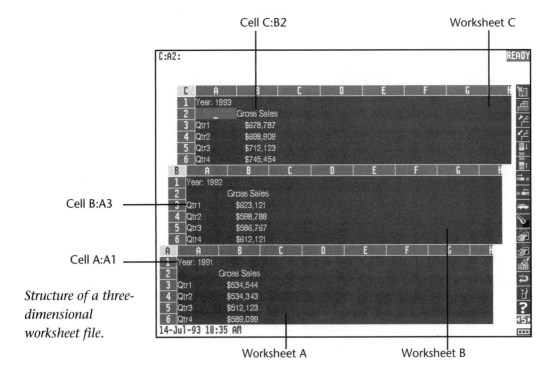

Structure of a three-dimensional worksheet file.

Some Terminology

When discussing three-dimensional worksheets, it's helpful to be clear on terminology. Things are complicated enough without additional confusion!

- ☛ A *worksheet file* is the unit that is saved to disk with the /File **Save** command, and retrieved from disk with /File **Retrieve**. A worksheet file can contain one or more worksheets.

- ☛ A *worksheet*, or *sheet* for short, is a single two-dimensional "page" in a worksheet file.

A worksheet file that contains only a single worksheet is, in effect, two-dimensional (like a single sheet of ledger paper). A worksheet file that contains multiple worksheets, sometimes called a *multi-sheet file*, is three-dimensional. Sometimes the term worksheet is used loosely to refer to a worksheet file when there's little chance of confusion.

Why Use Multi-Sheet Files?

You may think that the main advantage of multiple sheet files is that they provide a lot more room for your junk—er, I mean, valuable data. There is much more room in a multi sheet file, it's true. Their main advantage, however, is that they provide significantly greater flexibility in organization.

One use for multiple worksheet files is when you are coordinating similarly-formatted data from multiple sources. For example, suppose you are creating a worksheet that contains sales data from your firm's ten stores, as well as a summary of all data. By placing each store's data in its own worksheet, and then adding a summary worksheet on top, you can simplify your task greatly.

A second use is to help keep different kinds of material organized in complex projects. For example, raw data, summaries, graphs, and macros can each be kept in their own worksheets. This lessens the chance of errors, and makes it easier to keep things organized.

Cell Addresses in Multi-Sheet Files

In a multi-sheet file, each worksheet is identified by a letter that is displayed in the upper left corner of the worksheet frame (where the row numbers and column letters meet). The first 26 worksheets are A through Z, then double letters are used: AA through AZ, BA through BZ, and so on up to IV for the 256th and last worksheet. That's the maximum: 256 worksheets in a worksheet file. I've yet to see any worksheet file that contains anywhere near 256 worksheets, but it's nice to know they are available if you need them!

> ## By the Way . . .
> Here's a really impressive (though useless) bit of information. Each individual worksheet contains 256 columns and 8192 rows, for a total of 2,097,152 cells. A worksheet file with 256 worksheets contains 536,870,912 cells!

A cell in a worksheet file must be identified by its worksheet, as well as by its row and column. This is true even in a single-sheet worksheet file. A complete cell address, therefore, consists of its worksheet letter followed by a colon, the column letter, and the row number. Here are some examples:

A:C2	Sheet A, column C, row 2
AB:CD101	Sheet AB, column CD, row 101

In other parts of this book, I have been giving only the row and column parts of the cell and range address, assuming that you're always referring to the current sheet (sheet A in a single-sheet file). Of course, 1-2-3 always displays the complete three-part cell address in the control panel and in POINT mode, and I'll be doing the same in this chapter.

Adding and Deleting Worksheets

When you start a new worksheet file, it contains only a single worksheet, sheet A. Here's how to add additional worksheets:

1. Select /Worksheet Insert Sheet.

2. On the next menu, select **Before** or After to specify the position of the new sheet(s) with respect to the current sheet.

3. Type the number of worksheets to insert, then press **Enter**.

If you mistakenly delete a worksheet, you can get it back with the Undo command (**Alt+F4**).

When inserting new worksheets, the menu choices **Before** and **After** place the new worksheets either before or after the current sheet, in alphabetical order. For example, if the current worksheet is sheet A and you insert one worksheet before it, the new worksheet will be sheet A and the original worksheet will become sheet B. If you insert after, the new worksheet will be sheet B and the original worksheet will remain sheet A.

To delete a worksheet:

1. Move the cell pointer to any cell in the worksheet to be deleted.

2. Select /Worksheet Delete Sheet.

3. Press **Enter**.

By the Way . . .

If the worksheet file contains only one sheet, it cannot be deleted.

Moving in the Third Dimension

If your worksheet file contains more than one sheet, you need to be able to move the cell pointer from sheet to sheet. Here's how:

To move the cell pointer	*Press*
To the next sheet (for example, from A to B)	Ctrl+PgUp
To the previous sheet (for example, from B to A)	Ctrl+PgDn
To cell A:A1	Ctrl+Home

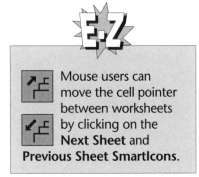

Mouse users can move the cell pointer between worksheets by clicking on the **Next Sheet** and **Previous Sheet SmartIcons.**

Three-Dimensional Ranges

When a worksheet file contains more than one sheet, you can define and name *three-dimensional ranges*, and use POINT mode in the same way you would with a regular two-dimensional range. A three-D range is a block that spans two or more adjacent worksheets; it must contain the same rows and columns in each worksheet. As you would expect, a three-D range is defined by the addresses of the cells at diagonally-opposite corners. For example, the range consisting of cells A1, A2, B1, and B2—in worksheets A, B, and C—has the range address **A:A1..C:B2.**

To use POINT mode with a three-D range, highlight the rows and columns in one worksheet, then press **Ctrl+PgUp** or **Ctrl+PgDn** to extend the range to other sheets. Here's an example: to erase all data in the range A:B2..C:D10,

1. Move the cell pointer to cell **A:B2.**

2. Select /**R**ange Erase.

3. Press → twice and ↓ eight times to extend the highlight to cell **A:D10.**

4. Press **Ctrl+PgUp** twice to extend the highlight to worksheet **C.**

5. Press **Enter.**

Group Mode

When you are working with a multiple-worksheet file, sometimes you'll want all the worksheets to have identical formatting, column widths, and so on. You can accomplish this easily by using *Group mode*. When you enable Group mode (which we'll get to in a minute), two things happen:

☛ First, all formatting and settings in the current worksheet (the one containing the cell pointer) are assigned automatically to all other worksheets in the file.

☛ Second, while Group mode is enabled, if you change any formatting or settings of any one of the file's worksheets, those changes are assigned automatically to all worksheets in the file.

Let's look at an example. Say you are working on a three-worksheet file, with Group mode disabled. In worksheet A, you change the width of column B to **15**, and change the format of cell B2 to **Currency**. If you then enable Group mode, here's what happens:

☛ The width of column B is changed to **15** in worksheets B and C.

☛ The format of cells B:B2 and C:C2 is changed to **Currency**.

Then, working in worksheet C with Group mode still enabled, you change the label alignment of cell C:C1 to **Centered**, and insert a new column between columns A and B. 1-2-3 will do these things automatically:

☛ Change the label alignment of cells A:C1 and B:C1 to **Centered**.

☛ Insert a new column between columns A and B in sheets A and B.

To enable or disable Group mode, select **/Worksheet Global Group**, then select **Enable** or **Disable**. When Group mode is enabled, 1-2-3 displays the GROUP indicator on the status line.

Keeping Things in Perspective

Normally you view only one worksheet of a multi-sheet file at a time. With *perspective view*, you can view three worksheets at once, as shown in the figure.

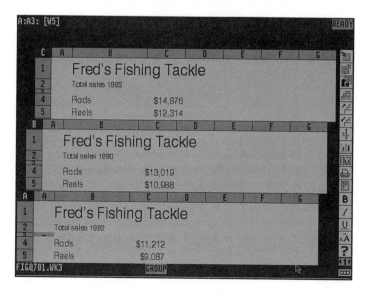

In perspective view, 1-2-3 displays three worksheets at one time.

Mouse users can enable and disable perspective view by clicking the **Perspective SmartIcon**.

To enable perspective view, Select /Work-sheet Window **P**erspective. To disable perspective view, select /Worksheet Window Clear.

By the Way . . .

In perspective view, scrolling in the active worksheet (the one with the cell pointer) causes the other worksheets to scroll as well, so the same rows and columns are always visible in all three.

The Least You Need to Know

Now that you have been "launched" into the third dimension, try to take these facts with you:

☛ A 1-2-3 worksheet file can contain as many as 256 individual worksheets. Think of each worksheet as a page in a book. A worksheet file starts out containing only a single worksheet; you add more worksheets as needed with the /Worksheet **I**nsert **S**heet command, and delete them with the /Worksheet **D**elete **S**heet command.

☛ To move the cell pointer from one worksheet to another, press **Ctrl+PgUp** or **Ctrl+PgDn**, or click on the **Next Sheet** and **Previous Sheet** SmartIcons: [08IC01] and [08IC02].

☛ When you work with multiple worksheets, you can use Group mode to apply the formatting and settings you used in one worksheet automatically to all other worksheets in the file. To enable or disable Group mode, select /Worksheet **G**lobal **G**roup, then select **E**nable or **D**isable.

☞ You can view three worksheets at one time using perspective mode. To enable perspective view, Select /Worksheet Window Perspective. To disable perspective view, select /Worksheet Window Clear.

This page unintentionally left blank.

Part II
Formulas and Functions

You won't see the real power of 1-2-3 until you start using formulas and functions. There's nothing tricky about these subjects—they're just the tools you use to manipulate your worksheet data to get the information you want.

The most important use of formulas and functions is to perform calculations on numbers in the worksheet. These calculations can be as simple as adding two numbers, or as complex as calculating depreciation.

Chapter 9
Formulas, Secret and Otherwise

In This Chapter

- ☛ What is a formula?
- ☛ Creating your first formula
- ☛ Formula operators
- ☛ Using parentheses

By now I hope you are beginning to get the hang of 1-2-3. You may not actually like it yet, but your hostility has lessened a bit (I hope!). You don't feel like such an idiot, and you may even have put your sledgehammer away! That's great, because we are starting to get to the good stuff now. Not that the earlier chapters weren't good, but now you're going to learn some things that will enable you to do some really neat stuff with 1-2-3.

So What's a Formula?

Formula may be a technical-sounding word, and I can almost hear some of you gritting your teeth. Aren't formulas something that your math teacher tried to force down your throat in 10th grade? No, it's nothing like that! Formulas are nothing more than a tool you use to get the answers you want from your 1-2-3 worksheets.

A formula is simply a way of combining numbers to get an answer that you need. Formulas are often very simple, as when you add your monthly rent to your utility bill to see how much money you need to leave in your checking account. You're also using a formula when you figure out the tip at a restaurant. Formulas can get more complicated than these examples, of course, but still they are nothing to fret about. If you want to fret about something, pick something important—like the economy, global warming, or whether the Cubs will ever win the World Series.

SPEAK LIKE A GEEK

Formula: An instruction that tells 1-2-3 to combine or manipulate numbers in a certain way, such as adding or subtracting them.

What Can Formulas Do?

With 1-2-3 you can create formulas to perform just about any sort of arithmetic you need. You can add numbers, subtract them, multiply, and divide. You can calculate averages, find logarithms, calculate loan payments, and more. But don't be intimidated by this. Formulas can be as simple or as complex as you want and need them to be. In your worksheets you'll use only the formulas you need; you can forget about the rest.

The best way to learn about formulas is to try them out, and that's just what we'll do in a minute. (To use formulas, you need to know about cell and range *addressing*. If you need to, please refer to Chapter 3 for information on cell addresses, and to Chapter 6 for information on ranges.)

Your First Formula

Well, it's time to buckle down and write your first 1-2-3 formula. No, you're not going to figure out the national debt or calculate the age of the universe, but it's a start! If you're at your computer, I suggest that you fire up 1-2-3 and follow along with me.

First, we will enter some numbers in cells A1, A2, and A3. The exact numbers don't matter, but let's be wildly creative and use 1, 2, and 3. Next, move the cell pointer to cell A4 and type in the formula +A1+A2+A3, then press **Enter**. Voilà! Cell A4 now displays **6**, which just happens to be the sum of the numbers in cells A1, A2, and A3. You've just entered your first formula, which tells 1-2-3 to add the values in cells A1, A2, and A3 and display the result. This is shown in the following figure.

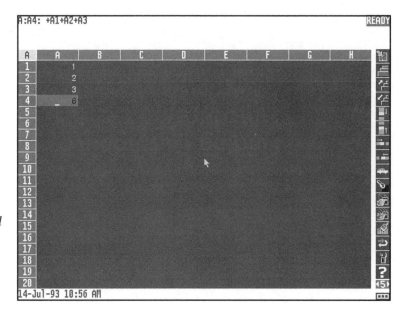

A formula in cell A4 displays the sum of the numbers in cells A1, A2, and A3.

Now let's try something else. Move the cell pointer to cell C2 and type in **+A1**, then press **Enter**. Cell C2 will display **1**, the same value that's in cell A1. This shows you that a formula does not always have to perform a calculation, but can also be used to "copy" a value from one cell to another. The formula +A1 tells 1-2-3, "Display whatever is in cell A1."

Finally, move the cell pointer to cell A1 and replace the 1 with the value **8**. There's no special trick to this—just type **8** and press **Enter**. What do you see? Cell A4 now displays **13**, which is the correct sum of the numbers in cells A1, A2, and A3. Also, cell C2 displays **8**, the current contents of cell A1. Your worksheet will appear as shown in the figure that follows.

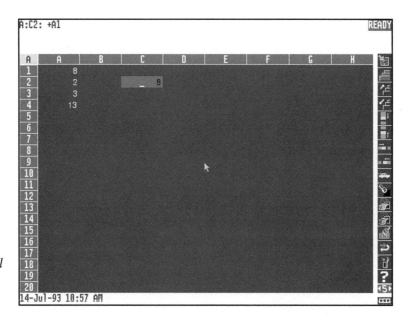

A formula in cell C2 displays the value in cell A1.

This shows you that whenever something changes in the worksheet, 1-2-3 updates all formulas automatically to take the change into account. Pretty neat, huh? Just try doing that with paper-and-pencil calculations. You'll have your eraser worn down to a nub in no time flat!

You may have noticed that a 1-2-3 worksheet displays formula results like any other number. In this worksheet, there's no way to look at cell A4 and tell whether the 13 displayed there is a regular old number, or the result of a formula. You *can* tell, however, by moving the cell pointer to the cell and looking at the control panel. If the cell does contain a formula, you will find it displayed in the control panel, as shown in the last two figures.

By the Way . . .

Remember that a formula can include any combination of cell references and numbers. **+A1+A2**, **+A1+25**, and **+100+25** are all valid formulas.

Hello, Operator?

All formulas use *operators*. No, not the telephone company folks! In 1-2-3, an operator is a symbol that tells 1-2-3 how to manipulate the values in a formula. A plus sign is one of 1-2-3's operators. All together, 1-2-3 has five operators that operate on numbers:

Operator symbol	Meaning
+	Addition
–	Subtraction
*	Multiplication
/	Division
^	Exponentiation

There's also one operator that operates on labels; this will be covered later in the chapter.

Operator Precedence

I know that *operator precedence* sounds like the name of a small town in Bulgaria, but it's not (at least as far as I know!). Rather, it refers to the relative importance that 1-2-3 assigns to the five arithmetic operators. Why is this important?

Look at the formula **+5+3*10**. There are two operators, and the result of the formula depends on which one is *evaluated* (that is, which operation is performed) first:

☞ If the addition **+5+3** is performed first, the formula becomes +8*10 and evaluates to 80.

☞ If the multiplication **+3*10** is performed first, the formula becomes +5+30 and evaluates to 35.

TECHNO NERD TEACHES

These five operators are sometimes called *arithmetic operators* because they perform arithmetic operations. Aren't you thrilled to know that?

SPEAK LIKE A GEEK

Exponentiation: Raising a number to a *power*. For example, 2^3 means "two to the third power," or 2 times 2 times 2.

Clearly, in a multiple-operator formula, the order in which the operators are evaluated can make a difference! Fortunately, 1-2-3 has a strict set of rules that govern this. Each operator is assigned a *precedence level*, as follows:

Operator(s)	Operation	Precedence level
^	Exponentiation	1 (highest)
* and /	Multiplication and division	2
+ and –	Addition and subtraction	3

Then, the following rules are observed:

☛ Operators with *higher* precedence are evaluated *first*.

☛ Operators with *equal* precedence are evaluated in *left-to-right order*.

Multiplication has higher precedence than addition, and is evaluated first. Therefore, the formula +5+3*10 will evaluate to 35.

Operator precedence: The order in which 1-2-3 evaluates arithmetic operators (that is, performs the operations they stand for) in a formula.

A Parenthetical Remark

What if the normal precedence order of formula evaluation won't work, and the wrong operation is performed first? For example, you want to divide the value in cell A1 by the sum of the values in cells B1 and C1. You might write +A1/B1+C1, but that won't work. Because the / operator has higher precedence than the +, the formula will *divide* A1 by B1, and *then* add the result to C1. What to do?

Fortunately, 1-2-3 has the solution. You can use *parentheses* to modify the evaluation order so that it suits your needs. When you include parentheses in a formula, anything inside parentheses is evaluated first, regardless of operator precedence. Continuing with our example, the formula **+A1/(B1+C1)** evaluates properly. The parentheses force the addition to be performed before the division.

> Parentheses must come in pairs, each "(" with a matching ")." If you try to enter a formula with one or more unmatched parentheses, 1-2-3 will beep, and switch to EDIT mode so you can edit the formula and correct the mistake.

There can be multiple pairs of parentheses in a formula, and parentheses can be *nested* (one pair inside another pair), as in **+A1^(B1/ (C1+D1))**. When parentheses are nested, evaluation always progresses from the *innermost* set outward. In this example, the + would be performed first, the / next, and the ^ last.

By the Way . . .

Even when parentheses are not needed to modify the order of evaluation, they can be useful if you want to make complex formulas easier to read and understand.

The Dreaded ERR

Once you start using formulas in your worksheets, you are sure to have the pleasure of entering a formula in a cell—and having the cell display **ERR** (error) instead of the formula result. Don't panic—this is just 1-2-3's way of telling you that it cannot evaluate the formula. The most common causes for this are:

- ☞ The formula contains a mathematically impossible operation, such as trying to divide by zero.

- ☞ The formula includes an undefined range name.

- ☞ The formula refers to another cell that displays ERR.

ERR: 1-2-3 displays this message in a worksheet cell containing a formula that cannot be evaluated.

Range Names in Formulas

You can use a range name in a formula just like a cell address. There's one possible problem, however. Formulas usually expect to work with single cells, and if you use a range name that refers to a multi-cell range, 1-2-3 will not be able to evaluate the formula, and it will display as ERR.

Here's an example. If the name TOTAL has been assigned to the single cell C5, then the formula +A1+TOTAL is exactly equivalent to the formula +A1+C5. If, however, the name TOTAL has been assigned to a multi-cell range, then the formula +A1+TOTAL is meaningless and cannot be evaluated.

Labels and Blank Cells in Formulas

When a formula refers to a cell that is blank (or contains a label), the cell is treated as if it contains 0. The only exception is a simple one-cell formula such as +A5, which evaluates to whatever is in cell A5. For example, if cell A5 contains the label **Sales**, then the formula

    +A5

evaluates to the label "Sales," and the formula

    +A5+10

evaluates to the value 10.

Concatenating Labels

Before you run off to find your dictionary, I'll tell you that *concatenating* means simply to combine two labels. For example, if you concatenate the labels "doo" and "fus" you get the label "doofus." 1-2-3's concatenation operator is &. If cell A1 contains "doo" and cell A2 contains "fus," then the formula +A1&A2 evaluates to the label "doofus."

Concatenation is useful when you want to create a label in one cell that is made up of two or more labels located in other cells. If you change the original labels, the concatenated label changes automatically. (Note that concatenation is considered a formula, just like the mathematical operations.)

Entering a Formula in the Worksheet

This is going to be a short section because there's not much to tell. Entering a formula is no different from entering a value or a label, except that a formula must start with either +, –, or (. That's how 1-2-3 knows it's a formula (and not a value or a label). You also edit formulas the same way you edit any other cell entry: move the cell pointer to the cell, and press F2 to enter EDIT mode (see Chapter 3 for details on editing cell entries).

Recalculation of Formulas

When you enter a formula in a cell, 1-2-3 immediately performs the calculations in the formula, and displays the result. What happens, however, if you change one or more of the values the formula uses? If the formula refers to values in worksheet cells, then changing those values will change the result of the formula. How does 1-2-3 handle this?

Left to itself, 1-2-3 recalculates all worksheet formulas automatically whenever data in the worksheet changes. This ensures that the results of all formulas are always up-to-date. If a worksheet contains a lot of formulas, however, automatic recalculation can slow things down considerably. You have the option of setting recalculation to manual, which means that 1-2-3 will recalculate the formulas in the worksheet only when you tell it to.

To enable manual recalculation, select /Worksheet Global Recalc Manual. When recalculation is set to Manual, 1-2-3 displays the **CALC** indicator in the status line whenever the worksheet needs to be recalculated. To recalculate manually, press **F9**.

> ## By the Way . . .
> You do not need to press F9 every time the CALC indicator is displayed—only when you want to update the worksheet's formulas.

To return to automatic recalculation, select /**W**orksheet **G**lobal **R**ecalc **A**utomatic.

The Least You Need to Know

Now you're all ready to "mix" your own formulas. Here are the basic points to remember:

- ☛ A formula uses the basic arithmetic operators + (addition), – (subtraction), * (multiplication), / (division), and ^ (exponentiation) to perform calculations of numbers stored in the worksheet. A formula can contain numbers, cell addresses, and range names.

- ☛ When a cell contains a formula, it displays the result of the formula. When the cell pointer is on the cell, however, the formula itself is displayed in the control panel.

- ☛ Formulas are typed into worksheet cells like any other entry. All formulas start with either +, (, or –.

- ☛ In a formula that contains more than one operator, the operations are performed in order of operator precedence, and in left-to-right order when precedence is equal. Parentheses can be used to alter the order of evaluation in a formula.

- ☛ Cells that contain a label or are blank are treated as zero in formulas.

- ☛ There's one operator that works with labels: the concatenation operator **&**, which simply combines two labels into a single label.

☞ 1-2-3 normally recalculates all formulas every time the worksheet is modified. To enable manual recalculation, select /**W**orksheet **G**lobal **R**ecalc **M**anual, and then press **F9** whenever you want to update the worksheet's formulas. Select /**W**orksheet **G**lobal **R**ecalc **A**utomatic to return to automatic recalculation.

This page unintentionally left blank.

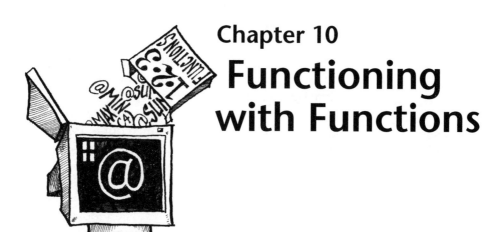

Chapter 10
Functioning with Functions

In This Chapter

- ☛ What is a function?
- ☛ How to use functions
- ☛ The most useful functions

The folks who created 1-2-3 were wise enough to realize that certain (common) calculations, or formulas, would be needed by a large proportion of the users. They thoughtfully included these formulas as part of 1-2-3.

What's a Function?

So what is a function? A *function* is nothing more than a formula that is built into 1-2-3. The nice folks at Lotus were kind enough to provide functions for many of the calculations that people need to do in their worksheets. As you'll soon see, using functions can save you lots of time and hassles.

Function: A formula that is built into 1-2-3. They are sometimes called "at" functions because their names all start with the "at" symbol (@): @SUM, @ROUND, etc.

Your First Function

Remember, a function is a built-in formula. You could write your own formulas to do all the things that 1-2-3's functions can do, but why bother? You or someone else paid good money for this program, and you might as well get as much out of it as possible!

The best introduction to using functions is to try one out yourself. Start 1-2-3, and enter the values **5**, **2**, and **6** in cells **A1**, **A2**, and **A3**. Then move the cell pointer to cell **A4**; type **@sum(A1..A3)**, then press **Enter**. You'll see that the cell displays **13**, which is the sum of the numbers in cells A1, A2, and A3, as shown in the following figure. Wasn't that easy? Let's take a look at the different parts of the function.

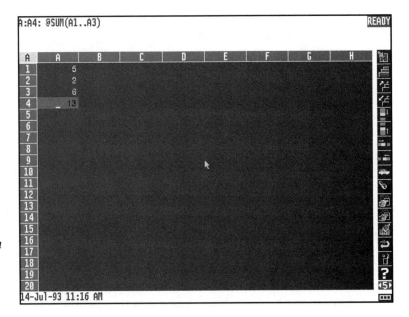

The @sum function in cell A4 calculates the sum of values in the range A1..A3.

Anatomy 101—The Parts of a Function

First there's the @ character. All functions start with this character—don't ask me why, that's just the way it is! In fact, the functions are sometimes called "at functions" because of this.

Next, there's the *function name*—in this case, **sum**. Each function has a name that indicates what it does (although some names are clearer than others). The **sum** function is clear enough—it calculates the sum of a bunch of numbers.

The final part is the *parentheses*—or, more importantly, what's inside the parentheses. This is called the *function argument*. As silly as the name sounds, it is nothing more than computer-talk for how you tell a function what to work with. In this case the argument is the range address **A1..A3** which tells the sum function to **sum** the numbers in cells A1 through A3.

Many functions require more than one argument, in which case they are separated by commas. A few functions take no argument at all (and like your mom, they certainly don't take any back talk!).

Argument: Information that tells a function what data to work with.

To get help on any particular function, type the function name (with the @ symbol) into a worksheet cell (don't press Enter), then press **F1**. The Help program starts, and goes to the @function section automatically. To view an index of all functions, press **F1** in READY mode, highlight **@Function Index**, then press **Enter**.

Types of Function Arguments

Some functions are intended to operate on numbers (also called *values*), while others work with labels (also called strings). Some arguments must be a single item, or cell, while others require a range. It's essential to use the proper type of argument. As with formulas, the argument of a function can be given as a numerical value, a cell address, a range address, or a range name. Let's look at some examples. For a list of 1-2-3 functions, see Appendix B of this book.

The function	Displays
@SUM(10,20,30)	The sum of the three numbers (60).
@SUM(SALES)	The sum of all values in the range named SALES.
@UPPER("Idiot")	The word with all letters converted to uppercase ("IDIOT").

continues

The function	Displays
@UPPER(A1)	The label in cell A1 with all letters converted to uppercase.
@AVG(B1..B10)	The average of all values in the range B1..B10.
@MIN(A1..A10,B6..B20)	The smallest value in the ranges A1..A10 and B6..B20.

The Dreaded ERR Returns

A cell that contains a function may display ERR. This means that 1-2-3 has encountered an error in evaluating the function—usually because the wrong type of argument has been used. For example, if you use a value argument with a function that requires a label argument, you'll get ERR displayed. Likewise, if you use a multi-cell range argument with a function that requires a single value, you'll also get ERR. Using an undefined range name as an argument is another way to get ERR displayed.

By the Way . . .

If you try to enter a function with the wrong number of arguments—or if you omit the comma between arguments, or the closing parenthesis—1-2-3 beeps, and enters EDIT mode so you can correct the mistake.

Functions in Formulas

Functions can be used alone, or can be included as parts of formulas. For example, if you wanted to calculate one-half of the largest value in the range A1..A10, you could use the formula

@MAX(A1..A10)*0.5

Or, if you wanted to divide the average of the values in the range named DATA1 by the sum of the values in the range C1..C20, you would write

@AVG(DATA1)/@SUM(C1..C20)

Functions can even be used as arguments to other functions. The following formula would calculate the square root of the sum of the values in the range D5..D15:

@SQUIRT(@SUM(D5..D15))

1-2-3 doesn't place any real limit on the complexity of formulas. Beyond a certain point, however, long complex formulas become difficult to understand and work with, even though they may operate correctly. Use your common sense, and keep formulas to a manageable size.

Getting the Point

When entering a function, you can use POINT mode to enter the addresses of single cells or ranges of cells. Here's how:

1. Type in the function up to the point where you need a cell or range address.

2. Use the **arrow** keys to move the cell pointer to the desired cell. As you move the cell pointer, 1-2-3 displays the current cell address in the function. To enter a single cell address, go to step 5. To enter a range address, continue with step 3.

3. Press . to anchor the range.

4. Use the **arrow** keys to expand the highlight to cover the desired range. As you do, 1-2-3 displays the range address in the function.

5. Continue typing in the function.

By the Way . . .
When you're in POINT mode, as indicated by the Mode indicator, you can select a range with the mouse. Point at the first cell in the range, press and hold the mouse button, and drag to the end of the range.

Let's look at a specific example. Here are the steps to enter the function @SUM(A1..A10):

1. Move the cell pointer to the cell where you want the formula.

2. Type **@SUM(** then stop (do not press **Enter**).

3. Use the **arrow** keys to move the cell pointer to cell **A1**.

4. Press **.** (period).

5. Use the **arrow** keys to move the cell pointer to cell **A10**.

6. Type **)**.

7. Press **Enter**.

Range Names, Anyone?

Functions can accept range names as arguments, and you can simply type them in—that is, if you can remember the proper name! There's an easier way:

1. Enter the function up to the point where you need the range name.

2. Press **F3**. 1-2-3 displays an alphabetical list of all the worksheet's range names.

3. Use the ← and → keys to highlight the desired name, then press **Enter**. 1-2-3 enters the highlighted name in the function.

4. Continue entering the rest of the function.

If 1-2-3 beeps when you press **F3** to get a list of range names, it means that there are no named ranges in the worksheet.

Finding Out About Functions

With over 100 functions, there's no way I can describe all of them here. You'll probably never use most of them, and you would certainly get bored pretty quickly! I will describe the most useful functions at the end of the chapter, but what about all those other ones? How can you find out if there's a function to perform just the calculation you need?

For quick information, you can turn to 1-2-3's on-line help. The Help system includes an @function index that provides an alphabetic list of all functions, with a brief description of each. To access the @function index, press **F1** while in READY mode, then select the **@Function Index** entry from the list of subjects displayed.

For more detailed information, you will have to use the 1-2-3 printed documentation. There's an entire chapter that presents an overview of the different categories of functions, as well as a detailed description of each one.

> **By the Way . . .**
> Recalculation of functions works the same way as recalculation of formulas. See Chapter 9 for details.

The Ten Most Useful Functions (According to Me)

This section provides brief descriptions of what I think are the ten most useful functions. You'll be able to perform lots of calculations in your worksheets with these functions. See Appendix B for a complete list of functions.

@SUM(RANGE)

The @SUM function calculates the sum of all values in the specified range. You can also use @SUM to add all the values in multiple ranges. Just list the ranges as arguments separated by commas: **@SUM(RANGE, RANGE2, RANGE3)**.

@AVG(RANGE)

The @AVG function calculates the *arithmetic average*, or mean, of all the values in the specified range. In other words, it adds all the values up and divides the sum by the total number of values. Blank cells in the range are ignored—but labels count as zeros, and can therefore throw the result off. This is really dumb, and the folks at Lotus should know better; @AVG should ignore labels, and use only value-containing cells in its calculation. But it doesn't, and there's nothing you or I can do about it. You'll just have to be careful (when using @AVG) to ensure there are no labels in the range.

@COUNT(RANGE)

The @COUNT function calculates the total number of cells in the specified range that contain data. Note that @COUNT counts every cell that contains anything: a value, a label, the ERR indicator, and so on. It ignores only empty cells.

@MAX(RANGE)

The @MAX function returns the largest value in the specified range. Label cells in the range count as zero; this matters only if the other values in the range are all negative (less than zero)—which would make zero the largest value, and cause @MAX to return an unexpected value.

@MIN

The @MIN function returns the smallest value in the specified range. This function has the same problem as @AVG—namely, that label cells count as zero, and can cause @MIN to return an unexpected value.

@NOW

The @NOW function takes no arguments; it returns the current date and time from your computer's clock (as a serial number). To have the value returned by @NOW displayed as a date or time, use one of 1-2-3's date or time formats. The value returned by @NOW is updated every time the worksheet is recalculated.

@ROUND(VALUE,PLACES)

The @ROUND function rounds off a numerical value to a specified number of decimal places. For example, the formula **@ROUND(A1,3)** rounds off the value in cell A1 to 3 decimal places. If cell A1 contains 4.97654221, then this formula displays **4.977**.

@NIT(VALUE)

The @NIT function returns the integer portion of its argument. In other words, it removes anything to the right of the decimal place. For example, **@NIT(10.89)** returns **10**.

@SD(RANGE)

The @SD function calculates the standard deviation of the values in the specified range. The standard deviation is a measure of how the individual values in the range differ from the average of all values in the range.

@MPH(AMOUNT,INTEREST,TERM)

The @MPH function calculates the payment on a specified loan. It's one of the more complex functions, but I've included it here because it can be very useful. It can tell you, for example, what the monthly payment on that new MBA will be.

The AMOUNT argument is the total amount of the loan. The INTEREST argument is the interest rate you must pay. TERM is the total number of payments. It's essential that the INTEREST and TERM arguments use the same time periods. Thus, if you are calculating monthly payments, INTEREST must be the per-month interest, and TERM must be the number of months in the loan.

Here's an example. You want to borrow $20,000 at an 8% annual interest rate, and pay it back over 60 months (5 years). You would write

@MPH(20000,0.08/12,60)

Note that the annual interest rate of 8% (or 0.08) must be divided by 12 to give the monthly interest rate. The answer is **405.5278**, which rounds off to a monthly payment of **$405.53**.

The Least You Need to Know

You're now ready to "function" at top efficiency (get it?). These are the most important things to remember:

☛ A *function* is a formula that is built into 1-2-3. There are over 100 functions that perform a wide variety of commonly-needed calculations.

☛ Each function has a *name* that describes its purpose. All function names start with @. You can view an alphabetical list of all functions, with a brief description of each, in the 1-2-3 Help system.

☛ Most functions take one or more *arguments*. An argument tells the function what data it is to use in its calculations. An argument can be a value or label. You type it directly into the function, into a cell or range address (which is more common), or a range name specifying where the data is located in the worksheet.

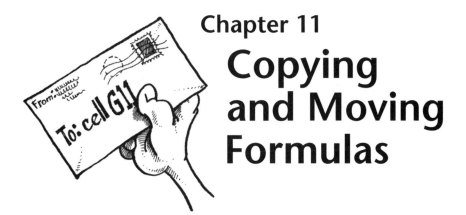

Chapter 11
Copying and Moving Formulas

In This Chapter

- Relative and absolute cell addresses
- Copying and moving formulas

You can use 1-2-3's Copy and Move commands to move and copy formulas from one location to another. In fact, this is a very powerful technique that you'll probably use a lot in your worksheets. There are, however, a few special things you must know when copying and moving formulas.

What's the Trick?

The answer is: there is no trick. You copy and move formulas in exactly the same way you copy and move other worksheet data, using the /Copy and /Move commands. So what's the problem?

The problem lies in the fact that formulas contain cell addresses. When a formula is copied, 1-2-3 treats its cell addresses in a certain way, depending on what the formula needs, and on the type of cell addresses. To use formulas effectively in your worksheets, you'll need to understand how this is done—and how to control it.

Everything Is Relative—or Is It?

When you use a cell address—either a single cell or a range address—in a formula, it is *relative* by default. This means that the address does not refer to a fixed worksheet location. Instead, the address refers to a location determined by the location of another cell (the one containing the formula). An example will make this clearer.

Let's say you have a worksheet with one column of values in cells A1..A10, and another column of values in cells B1..B10. You want to add the values in each column, so in cell A11 you enter the formula

@SUM(A1..A10)

Because A1..A10 is a relative address, it means "the 10 cells immediately above this cell" (remember, the formula is in cell A11). So far, so good.

What happens if you use the /Copy command to copy the formula to another cell? 1-2-3 changes the relative address automatically, so that it retains its original meaning ("the 10 cells immediately above this cell"). Thus, if you copy this formula from cell A11 to cell B11, the formula's range will be changed to B1..B10 (this is shown in the figure following)—and if you copy it to cell Z49, it will change to Z39..Z48. If you are copying between worksheets in a multi-sheet file, worksheet references are adjusted as well.

The formula @sum(A1..A10) was copied from cell A11 to cell B11. The relative cell addresses changed to B1..B10 to reflect the new location.

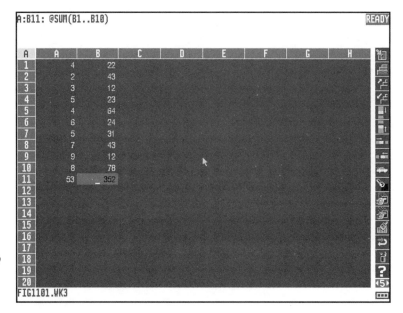

Relative cell addresses are appropriate for most 1-2-3 formulas (that's why they are the default, of course!). For example, you might have a dozen columns of numbers to sum. You can write the summing formula in the cell below one column, and then copy it to the cells below all the other columns (assuming the columns are the same length). The relative cell addresses will be adjusted so that each formula sums the column above it.

Relative cell address: An address that specifies a location relative to the cell containing the formula.

Absolute cell address: An address that specifies a fixed worksheet location.

When You're Absolutely Sure

There are times when you want a cell address to be *absolute*—that is, to refer to the same worksheet location, no matter where you copy it to. You can denote an absolute address by preceding the worksheet letter, column letter, and row number of the address with dollar signs ($). For example, **$A:C12** is an absolute address. It will remain exactly the same, no matter where the formula containing it is copied. The figure shows an example.

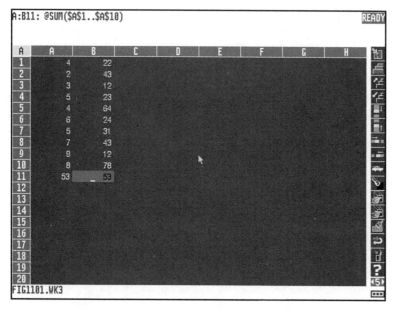

The formula @sum(A1..A10) was copied from cell A11 to cell B11. Because the cell addresses are absolute they were not changed to reflect the new location.

Mixed cell address: A cell address where some of the components (worksheet letter, column letter, and row number) are absolute, and some are relative.

What if you entered a formula with the wrong type of address—relative when it should have been absolute, or vice versa? No problem! Simply edit the formula to add dollar signs to (or remove them from) the address.

You can also create what is called a *mixed address*. Part of a mixed address is absolute, and part is relative. For example, A:$C12 is a mixed address. The column is absolute; the worksheet and row are relative. You can use any possible combination in a mixed address. When a formula containing a mixed address is copied, the absolute portions do not change, but the relative parts are modified to retain their original relative meanings.

Here's an example. The formula +$A5/2 is entered in cell B5. If it is then copied to cell C10, it will be changed to +$A10/2. The relative row reference was adjusted, but the absolute column reference was not.

Entering Absolute Addresses

You can enter an absolute or mixed address in a formula simply by typing the dollar signs in the proper locations when you type in the formula. You can also press **F4** to have 1-2-3 cycle automatically through the possible relative, mixed, and absolute addresses, as follows:

1. If you are entering a formula, type in the cell or range address (or enter it using POINT mode), then stop. If you are editing a formula, move the editing cursor onto the address.

2. Press **F4** one or more times, until the address has dollar signs in the desired locations.

3. Continue entering or editing the formula.

By the Way . . .

Be careful when entering absolute or mixed addresses. If your entry is inconsistent, such as @SUM(A1..A10), you may get inaccurate results when you copy the formula. Using the **F4** key to create absolute and mixed addresses eliminates the possibility of this problem.

A Moving Experience

What happens when you move a formula that contains an absolute cell address? Nothing. No adjustment is made to the address; the formula refers to the same worksheet cells after it is moved as it did before it was moved.

Moving data is a different story. If you use the /Move command to move data that is used in a formula (whether with a relative or an absolute cell address), the formula will be changed so the address refers to the same data in its new location.

Here's an example. Let's say that cell A11 contains the formula @SUM(A1..A10). You then move the data from A1..A10 to C1..C10. The formula is automatically changed to @SUM(C1..C10).

The Least You Need to Know

If you're going to be using the /Copy command to copy worksheet formulas, you "absolutely" need to remember the following "relatively" important points:

☞ A cell or range address in a formula is *relative* by default. That is, it refers to a location determined by the cell containing the formula. When a formula is copied to a different worksheet location, relative addresses are adjusted automatically to refer to the same location relative to the new cell containing the formula.

☞ You can make all or part of an address *absolute* by placing a dollar sign before the worksheet letter, the column letter, and/or the row number. When a formula is copied, absolute addresses (or the absolute parts of mixed addresses) are not adjusted.

☞ When entering or editing a formula, you can cycle a cell address between relative, mixed, and absolute by pressing **F4**.

This page unintentionally left blank.

Part III
Formatting and Printing

1-2-3 is often used not just as a tool for manipulating numbers, but also to generate reports and printouts that will be distributed to other people. Of course, you would like these reports to be attractive and professional-looking—that's where worksheet formatting comes in. And you have to get them from your screen to your printer, of course! These are the subjects of this section.

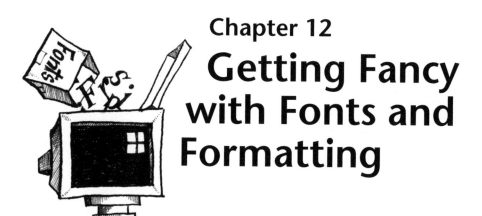

Chapter 12
Getting Fancy with Fonts and Formatting

In This Chapter

- 👉 Using different fonts
- 👉 Assigning different formats to values
- 👉 Label alignment options

A worksheet is full of information, and most of the information is displayed as text—letters, numbers, and so on. The way that the information is displayed has a large impact on the overall appearance and clarity of the worksheet.

1-2-3 offers a number of options for text display. You can control the typeface and size of text, the format used for display of numbers, and the way labels are aligned in their cells.

Fonts, Anyone?

Whenever 1-2-3 displays letters or numbers in a cell, it uses a particular *font*. The default font is something called "Swiss 12 Point," but there are many other fonts you can choose from.

Typeface: A particular design for printed and displayed characters.

Font: A typeface of a certain size.

Just what is a font? First of all, a font has a particular *typeface* which determines the overall shape and design of the individual characters (letters, numbers, and so on). Each typeface has a *name*; Dutch, Swiss, and Courier are examples of typefaces available in 1-2-3.

Second, a font has a particular *size* which reflects the height of the characters. Font sizes are measured in units called *points*, with one point equal to 1/72 of an inch.

Now you can understand what font names mean. The default font, "Swiss 12-Point" is 12 points high and uses the Swiss typeface. The figure below shows examples of the fonts that come with 1-2-3.

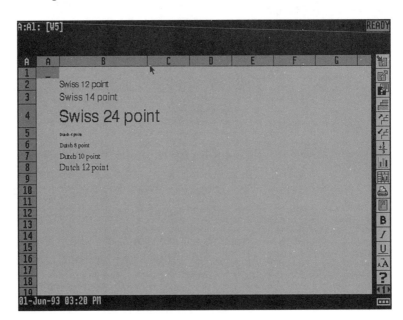

Some of the fonts available in 1-2-3.

Changing Fonts

Here's how to change the font used for data display in the worksheet:

1. Select :Format Font.

2. 1-2-3 displays a list of the available fonts. Press the number corresponding to the font you want to use.

3. Specify the worksheet range for the new font by typing in a range address and a range name (or by using POINT mode).

4. Press **Enter**.

> ## By the Way . . .
> When the cell pointer is on a cell whose font has been changed, the font name is displayed in curly brackets { } on the top line of the control panel.

It's Symbolic

You can display special symbols in your worksheet by using the *Xsymbol font*. The Xsymbol font does not contain the usual letters and numbers. Instead, it contains special symbols such as arrows and circled numbers. Each symbol in the set corresponds to a regular character (letter, number, etc.), and also to a numerical code between 33 and 126. You can find a list of all the symbols (as well as their corresponding characters and codes) in the appendix of your 1-2-3 Reference manual.

To cycle the current cell (or a preselected range of cells) through the available fonts, click on the Fonts SmartIcon:

To display a symbol in the worksheet:

1. Look up the character that corresponds to the symbol you want to display. For a large rightward-pointing arrow, for example, you would use the letter **T**.

2. Enter the character in the cell in the usual fashion.

3. Use the :Format Font command to set the cell's font to **Xsymbol**, with the desired point size.

Font Sets?

1-2-3 provides you with dozens of different fonts, but only eight of them can be used in a worksheet at one time. The eight fonts that are available are called a *font set*. (This is the list of eight fonts that 1-2-3 displays when you issue the :Format Font command). You can modify a worksheet's font set, making different fonts available for your data. Here's how:

To change all cells that use a particular font to a different font, it's a lot quicker to use the :Format Font Replace command to replace the old font with the new one than it is to use the :Format Font command to assign the new font to each cell individually.

1. Select :Format Font Replace.

2. 1-2-3 displays a list of the eight fonts in the current font set. Type the number of the font you want to replace.

3. A menu is displayed, showing four basic typefaces: Swiss, Dutch, Courier, and Xsymbol. Select the desired typeface for the new font. Or, select Other to display a list of additional typefaces from which you can select.

4. Type the desired point size for the new font, then press **Enter**.

When you modify a font set, all cells in the worksheet that used the old font (the one being replaced) are changed automatically to the new font.

By the Way . . .

The worksheet's default font is the one in position 1 in the font set. If you use the :Format Font Replace command to assign a different default font, you'll affect all the default cells in the worksheet.

Font set: A set of eight fonts available for use in a worksheet.

Getting Bold, and Other Font Attributes

The fonts that 1-2-3 uses can be displayed with a variety of font attributes. Cell entries can be displayed in boldface, in italics, or with underlining. You even have a choice of three underlining styles: single, double, and wide. The figure below shows some examples of font attributes.

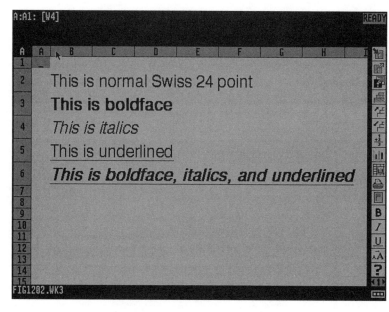

1-2-3 can display fonts in boldface, italics, or underlined.

To add or remove boldface from a range:

1. Select :Format Bold.

2. Select **S**et to add boldface to a range, or select Clear to remove boldface.

3. Specify the range by typing in a range address or range name (or by using POINT mode).

4. Press **Enter**.

You can change the font attributes of the current cell (or a preselected range of cells) by clicking on the **Bold, Italics,** or **Underlining SmartIcons:**

Font attributes: Qualities of (or changes to) the way text is displayed, including boldface, underlining, and italics.

To add or remove italics from a range:

1. Select **:Format Italics.**

2. Select **Set** to add italics to a range, or select Clear to remove italics.

3. Specify the range by typing in a range address or range name (or by using POINT mode).

4. Press **Enter.**

To add or remove underlining from a range:

1. Select **:Format Underline.**

2. To add underlining, select **Single, Double,** or **Wide.** To remove underlining, select Clear.

3. Specify the range by typing in a range address or range name (or by using POINT mode).

4. Press **Enter.**

By the Way . . .

You can combine font attributes in any way you like—single underlining with italics, for example, or boldface with wide underlining.

To assign Currency, Comma, or Percent format quickly, with two decimal places, click on the **Currency, Comma,** or **Percent SmartIcons:**

Gentlemen, Select Your Format

1-2-3 is primarily a tool for working with numbers, right? You would think, therefore, that you should have some control over the way numbers are displayed in the worksheet, and indeed you do!

1-2-3 offers a full range of *numeric formats* that control how numbers are displayed. The table describes the numeric formats you'll be using most often.

Format name	Result
General	No leading or trailing zeros.
Currency	Thousands separators, leading zero if needed, preceded by currency symbol ($).
Fixed	Leading and/or trailing zeros if needed.
Date	Displays date serial numbers; you can choose one of five standard date formats.
Percent	Displays values as percentages, with trailing percent sign.
, (comma)	Same as Currency, but without the currency symbol.

For all of the formats listed in the table (except General and Date), you can specify the number of digits to display to the right of the decimal point. The allowable range is 0–15.

By the Way . . .

1-2-3 offers several numeric formats that are not listed in this table. You can refer to the 1-2-3 documentation, or experiment for yourself, to see what they do.

To change the cell format of a range:

1. Select /**R**ange Format.

2. Select the desired format from the menu that is displayed.

3. Enter the desired number of decimal places, or (for Date format) select the specific format.

Thousands separators:
Commas placed every third
digit in large numbers, such
as 1,000,000.

Leading zero: A zero
displayed before the decimal point for numbers
between 1 and –1: for
example, 0.125.

Trailing zeros: One or
more zeros placed at the
end of a decimal number to
fill out the specified number
of decimal places: for
example, 1.5000.

4. Specify the range to format by entering a range address or range name (or by using POINT mode).

5. Press **Enter**.

When the cell pointer is on a cell whose format has been set with the /Range Format command, 1-2-3 displays an abbreviation of the cell's format, enclosed in parentheses, in the control panel. For example, **(F2)** is displayed for a cell formatted with **Fixed** format and **2** decimal places.

By the Way . . .

If you have a color monitor, you can display negative values in red. Select **/Range Format Other Color**, then select **Negative** to turn color on, or **Reset** to turn color off.

To reset a range's cell format to the worksheet global default, use the /Range Format **Reset** command.

Changing the Global Cell Format

The *global cell format* is the format that 1-2-3 uses for all worksheet cells whose format has not been changed with the /Range Format command. Normally, the global format is General, but you can change this if desired:

1. Select /Worksheet Global Format.

2. Select the desired global format from the menu that is displayed.

3. Enter the desired number of decimal places, or (for Date formats) choose a specific format.

4. Press **Enter**.

What's Your Alignment?

When you enter a label into a worksheet cell, it can be displayed one of three ways: left-aligned, right-aligned, or centered. The type of alignment is controlled by the *label prefix character* that 1-2-3 stores as the first character of each label:

' for left-aligned,

" for right-aligned, and

^ for centered (see Chapter 3 for details).

To change the alignment of all labels in a worksheet range:

1. Select /**R**ange **L**abel.

2. Select **L**eft, **R**ight, or **C**enter.

3. Specify the range to align by typing in a range address or range name (or by using POINT mode).

4. Press **Enter**.

Alignment not working? Remember that label alignment affects only those labels that are narrower than the cell they are in. A label that is the same width or wider is always displayed left-aligned.

> ## By the Way . . .
> You can specify a label's alignment when you first enter it by typing one of the label prefix characters as the first character of the label.

The /**R**ange **L**abel command affects only existing labels in the specified range. It has no effect on cells that contain values or formulas, and it does not affect labels that are entered subsequently. To modify the alignment of labels that will be entered in the future, you must change the global label alignment by selecting /**W**orksheet **G**lobal **L**abel, then selecting **L**eft, **R**ight, or **C**enter. Changing the global alignment has no effect on labels that are already in the worksheet.

To change the label alignment quickly for the current cell (or a preselected range of cells), click on the **Left**, **Center**, or **Right alignment SmartIcons** on Palette 2:

The Least You Need to Know

I hope you found this chapter to be *"font*astic." The proper use of fonts, symbols, attributes, and label alignment can make a big difference in the appearance of your worksheet. Here are the main points:

☛ The term *font* refers to the size and appearance of the letters and numbers used to display data in the worksheet. A worksheet can use as many as eight different fonts at a time. You use the WYSIWYG command **:Format F**ont to change fonts.

☛ A *font set* contains the eight fonts available to a worksheet at any one time. To change the fonts in the worksheet's font set, use the **:Format F**ont **R**eplace command.

☛ Any of 1-2-3's fonts can be displayed in boldface, italics, or with one of three underlining styles. To apply or remove these font attributes, use the **:Format B**old, **:Format I**talics, or **:Format U**nderline command, or click on the corresponding SmartIcon.

☛ 1-2-3 offers a variety of different cell formats for displaying numeric information. To assign a cell format to a range of cells, use the **/R**ange **F**ormat command. To change the worksheet's default cell format, use the **/W**orksheet **G**lobal **F**ormat command.

☛ You can select left, right, or center alignment for existing worksheet labels with the **/R**ange **L**abel command. To change the worksheet's default label alignment, use the **/W**orksheet **G**lobal **L**abel command.

Chapter 13

The Glamorous Worksheet: Borders, Shading, and Other Formatting

In This Chapter

- ☛ Adding borders and drop shadows
- ☛ Shading worksheet areas
- ☛ Copying formatting
- ☛ Using named styles

Getting Dressed Up to Go Out

When you create a worksheet that is going to "go out," that is, be printed or viewed by others, you'll want to make it as attractive as possible. In addition, you may want some way to emphasize certain parts of the worksheet, or call people's attention to certain tables or columns. You can do this very nicely by adding borders, drop shadows, and shading to the worksheet. This figure shows a worksheet with shading, borders, and a drop shadow applied.

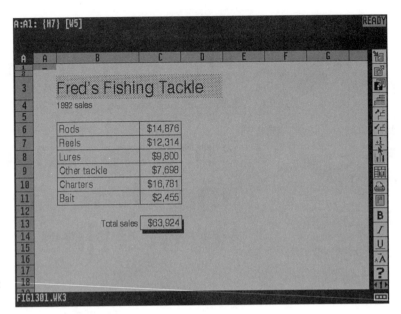

A worksheet with shading, borders, and a drop shadow.

Crossing the Border

When you add *borders* to a worksheet, you specify the range where the borders are to be placed. You have several options for border placement within that range, as shown here:

Border option	Draws a line...
Outline	Around the outside edge of the range.
Left	Vertically along the left edge of each cell in the range.
Right	Vertically along the right edge of each cell in the range.
Top	Horizontally along the top edge of each cell in the range.
Bottom	Horizontally along the bottom edge of each cell in the range.
All	Around all four edges of each cell in the range.

Here's the procedure for adding a single narrow border to a range:

1. Select :Format Lines.

2. Select the desired location for the border: Outline, Left, Right, Top, Bottom, or All.

3. Specify the range to which you want to add borders by typing in a range address or range name (or by using POINT mode).

4. Press **Enter**.

To add a double or a wide border, the procedure is slightly different:

1. Select :Format Lines.

2. Select Double or Wide.

3. Select the desired location for the border: Outline, Left, Right, Top, Bottom, or All.

4. Specify the range to which you want to add borders by typing in a range address or range name (or by using POINT mode).

5. Press **Enter**.

Here's how to remove borders from a range:

1. Select :Format Lines.

2. Select Clear.

3. Select the location that you want borders removed from: Outline, Left, Right, Top, Bottom, or All.

4. Specify the range from which you want to remove borders by typing in a range address or range name (or by using POINT mode).

5. Press **Enter**.

To cycle through the possible border settings for the current cell (or a preselected range of cells), click on the **Border SmartIcon on Palette 2:**

Dropping a Shadow

A *drop shadow* can be an effective device for setting off a cell or a range of cells. It looks best when combined with a border on the left and top edges of the range, as shown in the previous figure. With a drop shadow, the range looks as if it is raised above the worksheet surface—sure to attract attention! Here's how to add or remove a drop shadow.

1. Select :Format Lines Shadow.

2. Select Set to add a shadow, or Clear to remove it.

3. Specify the range by typing in a range address or range name (or by using POINT mode).

4. Press **Enter**.

Sitting in the Shade

The :Format Shade command is used to add *shading* to a worksheet range. You can choose between light gray, dark gray, and solid black shading. Here's how:

1. Select :Format Shade.

2. To add shading, select **Light**, **Dark**, or **Solid**. To remove shading, select Clear.

3. Specify the range by typing in a range address or range name (or by using POINT mode).

4. Press **Enter**.

> **By the Way . . .**
>
> When you use **S**olid shading, the text in the range will be hidden unless you use the :**F**ormat **C**olor **T**ext command to assign a color other than black to the text in the range.

Text of a Different Color

Data displayed in a worksheet is normally black. That's very proper and serious-looking, but you may want to liven up your worksheets with a little color! Here how to do it:

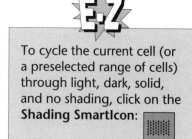

To cycle the current cell (or a preselected range of cells) through light, dark, solid, and no shading, click on the **Shading SmartIcon**:

1. Select :**F**ormat **C**olor **T**ext.

2. Select the desired text color from the list, or select **N**ormal to return text to the default color.

3. Specify the range where you want the new color to be used: type in a range address or range name, or use POINT mode.

4. Press **Enter**.

> **By the Way . . .**
>
> Changing text color works only if you have a color display (no kidding!). You'll get color in your printouts only if you're lucky enough to have a color printer.

Formatting Be Gone!

To remove all formatting from a range and reset all cells to the default font, follow these steps:

1. Select :Format **Reset**.

2. Specify the range to reset by typing in a range address or range name (or by using POINT mode).

3. Press **Enter**.

Formats to Go

There will be times when you have put a lot of work into getting the formatting of a worksheet range just right. If you want to use the same formatting for a different range, what do you do? It's difficult enough to remember all the formatting commands you used—and even if you can remember them, it's even more work issuing the same commands for a different range. Help!

1-2-3 comes to the rescue with the :Special Copy command. This command lets you copy all the formatting from one worksheet range to another. Only formatting is copied, not data. Here's how it works.

1. Move the cell pointer to the cell whose formatting you want to copy.

2. Select :Special Copy.

3. Press **Enter**.

4. Type in an address (or use POINT mode) to specify the range that the formatting will be copied to. This can be a single cell or a multi-cell range.

5. Press **Enter**.

By the Way . . .

The :Special Copy command copies only WYSIWYG formats—those applied with the :Format command. It does not copy regular 1-2-3 formats; those are applied with 1-2-3 commands such as /Range Format or /Range Label.

Name That Style

If you have created a format that you find attractive and think you may want to use again, you can save it as a *named style*. Once a style has been saved, you can apply it to any other worksheet range with a simple command. A worksheet can have as many as eight named styles saved at one time.

To create a named style, or to redefine an existing named style:

1. Move the cell pointer to a cell that has the formatting you want to save as a named style.

2. Select :Named-Style Define.

3. Select a number from 1–8 for the style you want to define or redefine.

4. Press **Enter**.

5. Type in a 1-to-6-character name for the style; use **Backspace**, if necessary, to erase the existing style name that is displayed.

6. Press **Enter**.

7. Type a style description (up to 37 characters long).

8. Press **Enter**.

To apply a named style to a worksheet range:

1. Select :Named-Style.

2. Select the name or number of the style you want to use. You can use the ← and → keys to highlight different style names; 1-2-3 displays the style description of the highlighted style on the third line of the control panel.

Named style: A collection of WYSIWYG formats that has been assigned a name.

If you redefine an existing named style, all worksheet ranges that were assigned the existing style will be reformatted automatically with the new style definition.

3. Type in an address (or use POINT mode) to specify the range you want the named style applied to.

4. Press **Enter**.

The Least You Need to Know

You'll wow them at your next presentation if you show worksheets that are "dressed up" using the techniques in this chapter. In summary:

☛ You can add a variety of *borders* to the cells in a worksheet range with the :**R**ange Lines command. You can choose between single, double, and wide borders. The same command can also be used to add a *drop shadow* to a worksheet range.

☛ To add light, dark, or solid *shading* to the worksheet, use the :**F**ormat **S**hade command.

☛ If your system has a color monitor, you can display worksheet data in different *colors* with the :**F**ormat **C**olor **T**ext command.

☛ The :**F**ormat **R**eset command can be used to remove all formatting from a worksheet range, and return it to its original "plain Jane" appearance.

☛ Duplicating the same formatting in different worksheet ranges is simple with the :**S**pecial **C**opy command, which copies the formatting (but not the data) from one worksheet range to another.

☛ If there are formatting styles you will use more than once, you can save them as *named styles* with the :**N**amed-Style **D**efine command. Once a style has been named and saved, you can apply it to other areas of the worksheet with the :**N**amed-Style command.

Chapter 14
Ready, Set, Print

In This Chapter

- Getting ready to print
- Printing all or part of your worksheet
- Changing page size, orientation, and margins

Getting Ready to Print

There are a few basics you should check before you try to print your worksheets. You may think these sound too simple even to mention, but overlooking them has tripped up some pretty smart people!

- First, is there a printer connected to your computer? Don't laugh—I know someone who complained bitterly that he couldn't get printouts, when in fact he had no printer (he later went on to become a lawyer). The printer may be sitting right next to your system—or, in the case of a network, it may be across the room or down the hall. Check with your local computer nerd if you're not sure.

☛ Second, the printer must be turned on, and *on line*. The term "on line" means simply that the printer is ready to receive data from the computer and print it. Most printers have an "on line" or "ready" light that is on when the printer is on line, and off when it is off line. There will also be a button labeled "on line" that you press to put the printer on line.

☛ Finally, the printer must have paper. I can't tell you how to load paper into your printer, but you may be able to figure it out. If you have problems, try standing there looking helpless, and maybe some kind soul will take pity and help you.

On line: A printer is said to be "on line" when it is ready to print.

Actually Printing

Printing all or part of your worksheet is actually quite easy. Even though there are many 1-2-3 print settings, you can usually ignore them because the default values are fine for most printing tasks. (You'll learn about the more important print settings later in the chapter; for now, don't worry about them.)

By the Way . . .

There is also a /Print command on the 1-2-3 menu, but the WYSIWYG **:Print** command is more flexible, so I suggest you use it.

All print-related commands start with **:Print**. When you issue this command, 1-2-3 displays the Print menu in the control panel, and the Print Settings dialog box on-screen (as shown in the figure).

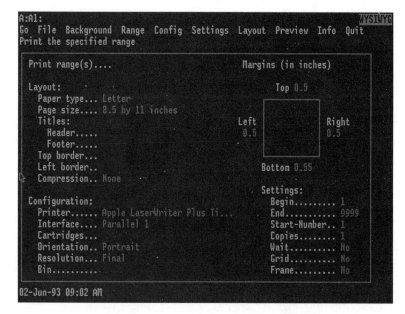

The Print Settings dialog box.

You can ignore most of the entries in this dialog box. You'll learn about some of them later, but for now, you need attend only to the **Print range(s)** entry in the upper left. This specifies the worksheet range that will be printed. It may be blank, or it may display a range address (if you specified a print range previously).

Assuming your printer is ready to go, here's how to print your worksheet:

Your Print Settings dialog box will be arranged differently from what you see in the figure, but it contains the same information. The Print commands you'll use are no different.

1. Select **:Print** to display the Print menu and the Print Settings dialog box. If the range you want to print is already specified in the **Print range(s)** section, go to step 5.

It's easy to see if there is a print range defined, because 1-2-3 displays a dotted border around the print range in the worksheet.

2. If there is an existing print range, select **Range Clear** to delete it.

3. Select **Range Set**.

4. Specify the range to print by typing in a range address or range name (or by using POINT mode), then press **Enter**.

5. Select **Go**. 1-2-3 will begin printing, and will display **WAIT** in the mode indicator while the print job is in progress. When the job is complete, you will be returned to READY mode.

By the Way . . .

Release 3.4 users can specify a three-dimensional print range in step 4 of this procedure. (You learned how to specify a three-dimensional range in Chapter 8; please refer there if your memory is a bit hazy.) 1-2-3 will print the worksheets in top-down order.

You can use POINT mode to select the entire worksheet quickly for printing. Just press **Home** to move the cell pointer to cell **A1**, press **.** to anchor the range, then press **End**, followed by **Home** to extend the range to the lower right corner of the active worksheet area.

A Sneak Preview

When you're working in 1-2-3 in WYSIWYG mode, the display on the screen shows you a pretty good approximation of what your final printout will look like. It doesn't show, however, the arrangement of data on the page, or the appearance of headers and footers. You can obtain an exact screen preview of what your printout will look like—without actually printing it—if you use the *preview* feature. (See following figure.) Using **Print Preview** can save time when you're fine-tuning the appearance of your report; it is a lot quicker than producing an actual print-out. It saves paper, too!

To use **Preview**, first set the print range as described earlier. Then select **Preview** from the **Print** menu. 1-2-3 displays a full-screen view of the first page of your printout, with all elements exactly as they will be printed.

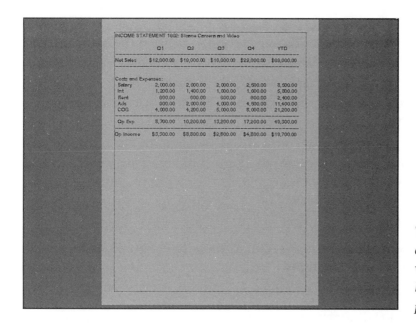

INCOME STATEMENT 1992: Sicnne Camera and Video					
	Q1	Q2	Q3	Q4	YTD
Net Sales	$12,000.00	$19,000.00	$16,000.00	$22,000.00	$69,000.00
Costs and Expenses:					
Salary	2,000.00	2,000.00	2,000.00	2,500.00	8,500.00
Int	1,200.00	1,400.00	1,000.00	1,000.00	5,800.00
Rent	600.00	600.00	600.00	600.00	2,400.00
Ads	900.00	2,000.00	4,600.00	4,500.00	11,400.00
COG	4,000.00	4,200.00	5,000.00	8,000.00	21,200.00
Op Exp	8,700.00	10,200.00	13,200.00	17,200.00	49,300.00
Op Income	$3,300.00	$8,800.00	$2,800.00	$4,800.00	$19,700.00

The :Print Preview command shows you what your report will look like when it is printed.

The dotted lines on the preview screen indicate the positions of the page margins. For multiple page reports, you can press **PgDn** or **Enter** to preview the next page, or **PgUp** to view the previous page. Press **Esc** to close the preview screen and return to the Print menu. If your preview seems just right, you can select Go to start printing. Otherwise, press **Esc** to return to READY mode where you can continue modifying the worksheet.

Changing Page Size and Margins

1-2-3's default paper size is 8-1/2 by 11 inch, which is the standard size used by most printers (sometimes called letter size). Depending on your printer, you may have the option of using a different page size (in fact, you may have to use a different size if your printer doesn't support letter size!). 1-2-3 has built-in definitions for several popular paper sizes, and also permits you to define a custom size. Here's how:

1. Select :Print Layout Page-Size. 1-2-3 displays a menu of the seven predefined sizes. If you press ← and → to move the highlight to different choices, the third line of the control panel will display a more detailed description of the highlighted size.

2. If you wish to use one of the predefined sizes, select it and go to step 7.

3. If you select Custom, enter the paper width, followed by an abbreviation of the units of measure: **in** for inches, **cm** for centimeters, or **mm** for millimeters. For example, enter **14in** for 14-inch-wide paper.

4. Press **Enter**.

5. Enter the paper length, again followed by the abbreviation for the units you are using.

6. Press **Enter**.

7. Select **Quit** to return to the Print menu.

By the Way . . .

If you enter a page size in centimeters (**cm**), 1-2-3 will automatically convert it to—and display it as—millimeters (1 cm = 10 mm).

Margin: Blank space between the edge of the page and the printed area.

On the Margin

1-2-3's default is to leave a margin of 0.5 inch at the top, left, and right edges of the page, and a margin of 0.55 inch at the bottom. These settings are fine for most print jobs, but you can modify them. Here are the steps to follow:

1. Select :Print Layout Margins.

2. Select Left, Right, Top, or Bottom.

3. Type in the desired margin size, followed by an abbreviation of the units of measure: **in** for inches, **cm** for centimeters, or **mm** for millimeters. For example, enter **2cm** for a 2-centimeter margin.

4. Press **Enter**.

5. Select another margin to change, or select Quit twice to return to the Print menu.

Portrait or Landscape?

The terms *portrait* and *landscape* sound like they have more to do with painting than with computers—and that, in fact, is where they have their origin. In computer-ese these terms are used to describe the way paper is oriented during printing. Portrait orientation prints with the long edge of the paper vertical, while landscape orientation has the paper rotated one-quarter turn so the long edge is horizontal. Portrait orientation is most common, and is fine for many worksheet print jobs. Landscape orientation can be useful when you want to fit as many columns on each page as possible.

The current paper orientation setting is displayed in the Configuration section of the Print dialog box. Here's how to change the setting:

1. If necessary, select :Print to display the Print menu.

2. Select Config Orientation.

3. Select Portrait or Landscape.

4. Select Quit to return to the Print menu.

Not all printers have the ability to print in landscape orientation. If you're having trouble getting landscape-orientation jobs to print, this may be the reason. Check your printer documentation.

Portrait orientation: The long edge of the paper is vertical.

Landscape orientation: The long edge of the paper is horizontal.

Using Headers and Footers

A *header* is a line of text that is printed at the top of every page in your printout. Likewise, a *footer* is—you guessed it!—a line printed at the bottom of every page. Headers and footers can contain identifying information (such as your name or the company name), and can also include page numbers and the date.

To add a header or footer to your report:

1. Select **:Print Layout Titles**, then select either **Header** or **Footer**. The existing header or footer text, if any, is displayed in the control panel.

2. If necessary, press **Backspace** to erase the existing text. Enter the header or footer text; special symbols you can use appear in the paragraph following.

3. Press **Enter**.

4. Select **Quit** twice to return to the Print menu.

By the Way . . .

You can use the contents of a worksheet cell as the header or footer: place the cell address, preceded by \, in the header or footer text. For example, if you enter **B6** for the header, whatever is in cell B6 will be printed as the header.

A header or footer can be as long as 512 characters, but only the part that fits on the page will actually be printed. The following special characters can be placed in a header or footer:

\#   The page number

@   Today's date

You can also use the vertical pipe character (|) to divide the header or footer into left-aligned, centered, and right-aligned portions:

- ☞ Text before the first | character is left-aligned.

- ☞ Text after the first | but before the second | is centered.

- ☞ Text after the second | is right-aligned.

Let's look at a couple of examples. The header text

|#

will produce a header consisting only of a centered page number. The header text

@|Prepared by J. Smith|#

will produce a header with the date left-aligned, "Prepared by J. Smith" centered, and the page number right-aligned. The header text

||\C12

will produce a header consisting of the contents of cell C12, right-aligned.

Use the :**P**rint **P**review command to see exactly what your headers and footers will look like.

By the Way . . .

Headers and footers are printed just below or above the page margin, with two blank lines between the header or footer and the printed data.

The Least You Need to Know

You're now ready to "print 'til you drop!" Before you do, be sure to keep these important points in mind:

☞ Before you can print a single page, you must have a printer connected to your computer. The printer must be turned on, on line, and it must have paper.

☞ To print all or part of your worksheet, use the **:Print Range** command to specify the range to print, then select the **Go** command to start printing.

☞ Want to save time and paper? Use the **:Print Preview** command for a screen preview of exactly what your printed report will look like.

Part IV
Getting Graphical

It has been said that a picture is worth a thousand words (probably by an artist who was trying to sell a painting!). This may be an overused, trite saying, but there is an element of truth to it. The right picture can indeed be a very effective communication device. 1-2-3 can display and print a special kind of picture called a graph. Graphs provide a powerful tool for presenting and summarizing numerical information, and they can turn a boring report into something that is . . . well, not quite as boring! This section shows you how to use graphs in your worksheets and printed reports.

Chapter 15
Graphs From the Ground Up

In This Chapter

- The parts of a graph
- Creating a basic graph
- Assigning names to graphs
- Creating quick graphs

Much of 1-2-3's power comes from its ability to create graphs quickly (and almost without effort) from data in the worksheet. This chapter shows you the basics of 1-2-3 graphs, including the parts of a graph and how to create a basic graph.

Graph Basics

If we're going to learn about graphs, it will help to know what the various parts of a graph are called. I won't get very far referring to "that doohickey" and "the thing-a-ma-bob." The figure below shows a 1-2-3 graph with its parts labeled.

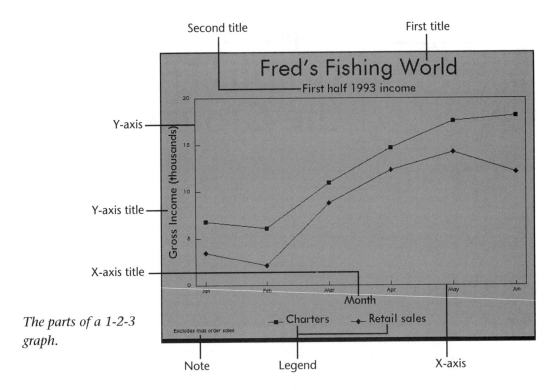

The parts of a 1-2-3 graph.

Some of the graph features shown in this figure, such as the titles and legend, are graph *options* that are covered in Chapter 17. The basic graphs you'll learn to create in this chapter are a lot simpler, but hey, it's a start!

Data, Data Everywhere

All graphs plot data, but what kind of data? There are two basic types of data that a graph can plot, and they correspond to the two types of data that can be placed in the worksheet.

- ☛ *Numeric data* is represented by numbers, or values, in the worksheet. All graph types plot numeric data on the Y-axis, and one graph type also plots numeric data on the X-axis.

- ☛ *Category data* is represented by labels in the worksheet. All graph types except one plot category data on the X-axis.

> ## By the Way . . .
> There's one kind of graph, called a *pie chart*, that doesn't have an X-axis or a Y-axis. You can learn about pie charts in Chapter 16.

Is That Data in Range?

How do you tell 1-2-3 which worksheet data to include in a graph? As you might expect, you do so with ranges. Each graph has a number of data ranges. There's one range, called the *X data range*, for the data that is to be plotted on the X-axis. There are six data ranges, called *data ranges A through F*, for data that is to be plotted on the Y-axis (you don't have to use all six Y data ranges). By specifying the worksheet range that is to be associated with each of the graph's data ranges, you control the data that the graph displays.

With rare exceptions (which we won't worry about) worksheet data to be graphed is arranged in adjacent rows or columns. Since this is the way that worksheet data is normally arranged, everything works out fine! The following figure shows two ways in which the same data could be arranged in the worksheet for graphing; the next figure shows the resulting graph.

Numeric data: Data that is represented by numbers, or *values*, in the worksheet.

Category data: Data that is represented by labels in the worksheet.

Does some (or all) of the data seem to be missing from the graph you're displaying? You've probably made an error entering the data ranges, specifying empty worksheet cells instead of the actual data location.

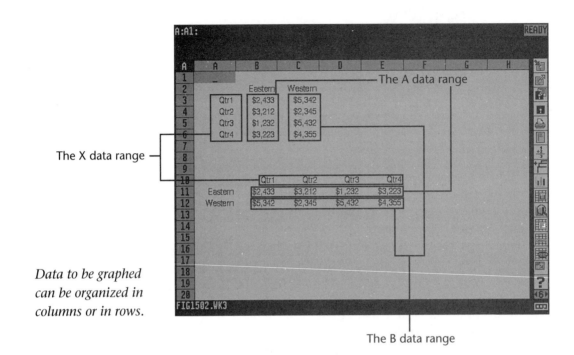

Data to be graphed can be organized in columns or in rows.

The X data range

The A data range

The B data range

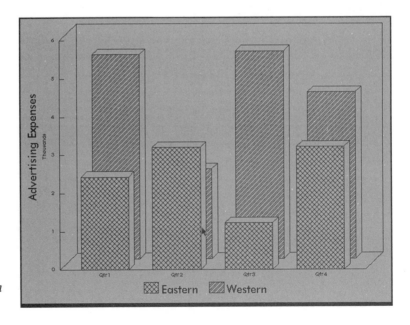

A graph of the data in the previous figure.

> ### By the Way . . .
> Except under special circumstances, each data range in a graph should contain the same number of cells as all other data ranges.

Your First Graph

Most people find that actually creating a graph is simpler than it sounds! Before going into more detail on some graph commands, let's run through the procedure for creating a simple line graph. Start with a blank 1-2-3 worksheet; type in the data shown in the figure, using the range from **A1** to **C4** (Don't worry about what the data means!)

Save yourself trouble—if at all possible, keep all data for a given graph in the same area of the worksheet.

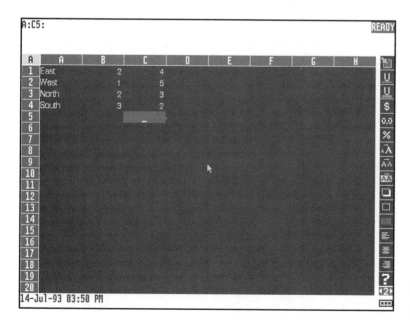

Your worksheet after entering data for your first graph.

Now follow these steps:

1. Select /Graph to display the Graph menu.

2. Select **X** to specify the X data range. Specify the range **A1..A4** (either by typing in the range address or by using POINT mode), then press **Enter**.

3. Select **A** to specify the A data range. Specify the range **B1..B4**, then press **Enter**.

4. Select **B** to specify the B data range. Specify the range **C1..C4**, then press **Enter**.

5. Select **View** to display the graph. Your graph should look like the following figure.

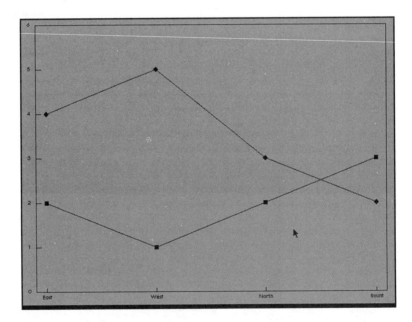

Your first graph should look like this.

That was pretty easy, wasn't it? The graph that you see is called a *line graph*, which is one of 1-2-3's seven graph types. (See Chapter 16 for information on the different graph types and how to display them.) Of course, the graph you created is rather basic, but let's not rush things! You'll learn about using graph options in Chapter 17.

> **By the Way . . .**
>
> Each data range should be a range of cells in a single column or a single row. 1-2-3 does not prevent you from defining graph data ranges that span two or more rows or columns, but the results will be unpredictable.

Typecast Your Graphs

1-2-3 offers seven different types of graphs, with two or more variations on most of them. The line graph you've seen earlier in this chapter is one of the graph types. Another type is a *bar graph*. (Chapter 16 explains the different graph types, and shows examples of each.)

While in READY mode, you can display the most recent graph (called the *current graph*) by pressing **F10** or by clicking on the

Graph SmartIcon:

You specify the type of graph you want with the /**Graph Type** command. If you don't specify a type, 1-2-3 will create a line graph. You specify a graph type when you are first designing a graph, and you can also change the type of an existing graph at any time. When you change the type of a graph, all the other graph settings remain unchanged. This makes it easy to create a graph, then try it out as different types to see which type is best suited to the data.

Current graph: The graph that was most recently displayed.

A Recipe for Graphs

Because each graph is different, there is no single sequence of steps to follow to create a graph. The following is about as close as I can come to a recipe for graphs:

1. Select /**Graph** to display the Graph menu.

2. To be sure you are starting with a clean slate, select **Reset Graph** to clear any previous graph settings.

3. Select **Type**, then choose the desired graph type (unless you want the default line graph).

4. Select **X**, specify the X data range by typing in a range address (or by using POINT mode), then press **Enter**.

5. Select **A**, specify the A data range by typing in a range address (or by using POINT mode), then press **Enter**.

6. If your graph will have more than one data range plotted on the Y-axis, repeat step 4 as needed to specify the B data range, the C data range, etc.

7. If desired, select **Options** to set various graph options (see Chapter 17). When you are finished setting options, select **Quit** from the Options menu to return to the Graph menu.

8. If desired, select **Type Features** to select graph features (see later in this chapter). When you're finished setting features, select **Quit** from the Features menu to return to the Graph menu.

9. Select **View** to display the graph on the screen. When you're done viewing the graph, press **Esc** to return to the graph menu. You can then continue modifying the graph; and press **Quit** to return to READY mode.

I Didn't Catch Your Name

At any moment, there can be only a single current graph in a 1-2-3 worksheet file. This is the graph that was most recently displayed. If you create a new graph, the original graph will be lost—gone forever!

Chances are you will be creating and displaying lots of different graphs in your worksheet. It would be a real drag if you could have only a single graph defined at a time. Fortunately, this is not the case. 1-2-3 lets you assign a *name* to each graph you create. Once a graph has been named, all its settings are stored, and the graph can be quickly recalled with a simple command.

To assign a name to the current graph:

1. In READY mode, press **F10** to view the graph to be sure its appearance is correct. Press **Esc** to return to READY mode.

2. Select /Graph Name Create.

3. Enter a name for the graph; it can be up to 15 characters long. (Or, if you are redefining an existing graph name, press → and ← to highlight the graph name in the list that is displayed.)

4. Press **Enter**.

5. Select **Quit** to exit the Graph menu.

When you name a graph, all the graph settings—data ranges, graph type, options, etc.—are stored in association with the name. When you save the worksheet with the /File **Save** command, all named graph settings are saved with it. There is no limit to the number of named graphs that a worksheet can contain.

By the Way . . .

While creating a complex graph, occasionally you should use the /Graph **Name** **Create** command to name the graph (using the same name each time, of course), and use the /File **Save** command to save the worksheet. This way you won't lose all your work in the event of a power outage or system crash.

To display a named graph:

1. Select /Graph Name Use.

2. Type in the desired graph name, or select it from the list using the → and ← keys.

3. Press **Enter**.

By the Way . . .

If you display a named graph and then make modifications, the changes are *not* saved automatically. You must use the /Graph **Name** **Create** command to redefine the old graph name with the new graph settings.

To delete named graphs:

1. Select /Graph Name.

2. To delete all named graphs, select **Reset**. To delete a single named graph, select **Delete**, press → and ← to highlight the graph name, then press **Enter**.

By the Way . . .

If you modify the worksheet data that a graph uses, they are reflected in the graph automatically the next time you display it.

Feature That!

If you select Type from the **Graph** menu, you'll see a menu listing 1-2-3's seven graph types. The menu's last entry seems strange, however—it is Features, which hardly sounds like a type of graph. And indeed it is not; rather, the Features command leads to another menu which you use to control a variety of graph "features." These settings control the way the graph is displayed. The features you will use most often are described (rather briefly) here. I suggest you experiment with the Features settings to get a better feel for what they do.

- ☛ Vert: Displays the graph in the normal orientation, with the X-axis horizontal and the Y-axis vertical. This is the default.

- ☛ Horiz: Displays the graph rotated 90 degrees so the Y-axis is horizontal and the X-axis is vertical.

- ☛ Stacked: Displays two or more data ranges, one on top of the next. Use only with line, bar, mixed, or XY graph types.

- ☛ 100%: Plots each data point as a percent of the largest value in the data range. Use only with line, bar, stacked bar, mixed, and XY graph types. For example, if the data range contains the values 2, 4, 6 and 8, they will be plotted as 25%, 50%, 75%, and 100% respectively.

☛ Frame: Controls the display of a *frame*, or border, around all or part of a graph. You have the following frame position options: All, **Left**, **Right**, **Top**, **Bottom**, and **None**.

☛ 3D: Displays any graph type (except HLCO) in a three-dimensional perspective.

By the Way . . .

The **Frame** command was surely designed by a committee. To get a border around only part of the graph, you must first select **All** to place a border around the entire graph, then select **Left**, **Right**, **Top**, and/or **Bottom** to remove the border from the indicated position(s).

Graphs in a Hurry

If your data is organized properly in the worksheet, you can create a basic graph almost instantly using 1-2-3's Quick Graph feature. The rules for data organization are as follows:

☛ The data must be in adjacent rows or columns in a single worksheet.

☛ The first row or column must contain data for the X data range.

☛ The second row or column must contain data range A, the third row or column data range B, and so on up to a maximum of 7 total rows or columns.

☛ *Optional:* Except for optional labels directly above or to the left, the range must be separated from other worksheet data on all sides by at least two empty rows and columns.

Then, the procedure for creating a Quick Graph is as follows:

1. If you've already used empty rows and columns to separate the range from other worksheet data, simply place the cell pointer anywhere in the range. If you have not separated the range, you must preselect (highlight) it.

2. Click on the **Graph SmartIcon**.

3. 1-2-3 displays the Quick Graph dialog box, as shown in the figure.

4. The most important setting in this dialog box is **Data ranges in**. Select **Columns** or **Rows**, depending on how your data is arranged in the range.

5. Change other Quick Graph option settings as needed, then select **OK** to display the graph.

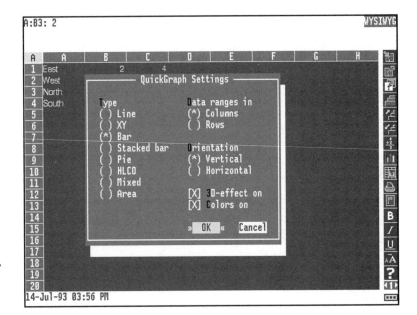

You make Quick Graph settings in the Quick Graph dialog box.

The Least You Need to Know

I think you'll agree that graphs are perhaps the best part of 1-2-3. If you remember the following points, your friends will soon be calling you the "graph guru."

☞ 1-2-3 can display graphs of your worksheet data. Graphs are powerful tools for data presentation, and can improve the clarity and impact of your reports significantly.

☞ A graph can represent two types of data: *numeric data* (values) and *category data* (labels). Each graph plots one range of data on the X-axis, and between one and six ranges of data on the Y-axis.

☞ All graphic commands are found on the Graph menu, which is displayed by selecting /**G**raph. On this menu, you use the **X** and the **A** through **F** commands to specify the graph's data ranges, the **V**iew command to display the graph, and the **T**ype command to change the type of the graph.

☞ Graph features let you control various aspects of how your graph is displayed, such as the frame around the graph and the use of a three-dimensional perspective. To set graph features, select /**G**raph **T**ype **F**eatures.

☞ On the **Graph** menu, select Name Create to assign a name to the current graph and save its settings. Select Name Use to display a named graph.

☞ To display a Quick Graph, arrange your data in adjacent rows or columns, then click on the **Graph SmartIcon**.

This page unintentionally left blank.

Chapter 16

Graph, Are You My Type?

In This Chapter

- ☞ 1-2-3's seven graph types
- ☞ When to use each type of graph
- ☞ Special graph options

1-2-3 provides seven, count 'em, *seven* different graph types. Each type of graph displays data in a different way, and is best suited for presenting certain kinds of data. This chapter describes each type of graph, shows an example, and gives you some tips on what kinds of data work best with each graph type. These tips are just suggestions, however, not rules. For your own data, you should experiment to determine which graph types get your message across best.

You learned how to select a graph type in the previous chapter. To refresh your memory, you select /Graph Type, then select the desired type. You can do this before or after specifying other graph settings.

Keeping Your Data in Line

A *line graph* plots data with lines and symbols. Each Y data range is plotted as a line, and each individual data value in the range is plotted as a symbol on the line. When a line graph contains two or more Y data ranges, the different ranges are distinguished by different colors and different symbol shapes.

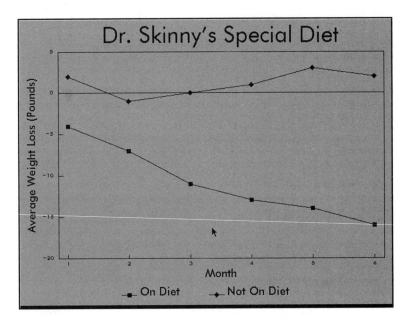

A line graph.

> ## By the Way . . .
> Line graphs are well suited for showing changes occurring over time.

Changing Line Graph Format

There are certain formatting options that apply specifically to line graphs. These options control how the Y data series is displayed.

1. From the **Graph** menu, select Options Format.

2. Select **A** through **F** to specify the data range whose format you want to change, or select Graph to change the format for all data ranges in the graph.

3. Select one of the following format options:

 ☞ Lines: Displays a line only.

 ☞ Symbols: Displays symbols only.

 ☞ Both: Displays both lines and symbols (this is the default).

 ☞ Neither: Displays neither lines nor symbols, effectively hiding the data range.

 ☞ Area: Fills the area between the lines with solid colors.

4. Select **Quit** twice to return to the Graph menu.

The Best Graphs, Bar None

A *bar graph* uses different sized bars to represent individual data points. In a bar graph with two or more Y data ranges, each data range is represented by bars displayed with a particular color or pattern.

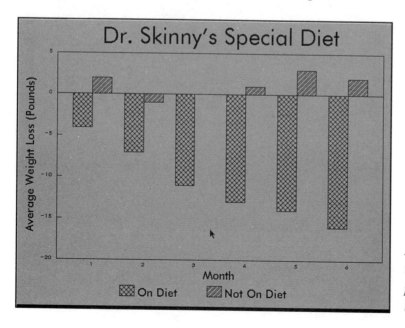

A bar graph, plotting the same data as was plotted in the previous line graph.

Stack Your Data

A *stacked bar graph* is similar to a bar graph except that the individual bars in each group are stacked on top of each other instead of being displayed side-by-side. A stacked bar graph is possible only when there are at least two Y data ranges.

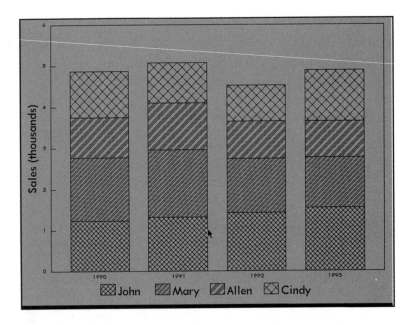

A stacked bar graph.

Why Ask Why? XY!

An *XY graph* is sometimes referred to as a *scatter graph*. This is the only one of 1-2-3's graph types that plots values, and not categories, on the X axis. This type of graph is used to display the correlation between pairs of numeric values. For example, a farmer could measure his annual crop yield per acre and plot it against the total rainfall. By using the yield as the Y data range, and the rainfall values as the X data range, he could create a graph showing the fact that greater rainfall tends to result in larger crops.

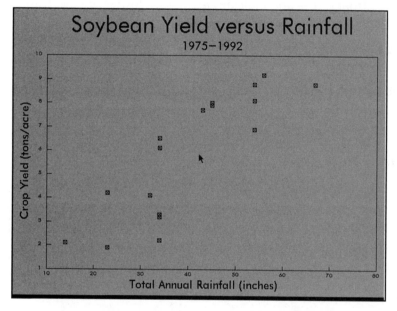

An XY graph.

An XY plot looks best if you plot symbols only for each data point. To do this, from the **Graph** menu select Options Format Graph Symbols Quit Quit.

By the Way . . .

The XY graph is the only type that can be used to plot values against values.

HLCO—What Kind of Name Is That?

HLCO stands for *high-low-close-open*, a special type of graph designed for plotting stock market data. Each symbol on the graph consists of a vertical line with two horizontal *tick marks*, and represents four items of information about a stock's price for the specified period:

- ☞ The top of the line indicates the stock's highest price during the period.

- ☞ The bottom of the line indicates the stock's lowest price during the period.

- ☞ The left tick mark indicates the stock's opening price at the start of the period.

- ☞ The right tick mark indicates the stock's closing price at the end of the period.

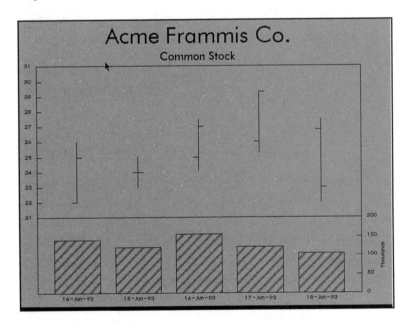

An HLCO graph.

The high, low, close, and open figures are specified by the A, B, C, and D data ranges respectively. If you include a data series E it is plotted as a bar graph below the HLCO section of the graph; this is used traditionally to display trading volume for the stock (as shown in the figure). If you specify a data series F, it is plotted as a line superimposed on the HLCO graph (not illustrated).

By the Way . . .

While HLCO graphs are used most commonly for stock market data, they can be used for any quantity that varies over fixed time periods: water pressure, temperature, and so on.

In Mixed Company

A *mixed graph* is a combination of a line graph and a bar graph in a single graph. Data series A, B, and C are plotted as bars, and data series D, E, and F are plotted as lines.

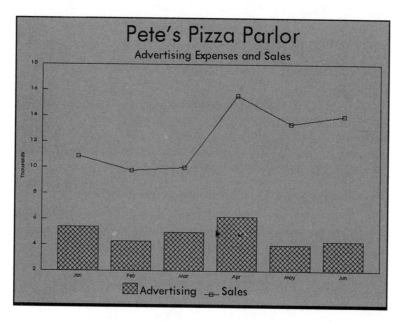

A mixed graph.

By the Way . . .

Use a mixed graph type to compare different types of data, or to provide a different appearance for your graphs.

A Pie in the Face

A *pie graph* is unique among 1-2-3's graph types in that it can plot only a single Y data series (the A data range). The sum of all values in the Y data series is represented by a circle (the "pie"), and each individual value is represented by a wedge (a "slice of pie"). The size of each wedge reflects the value's relative contribution to the total.

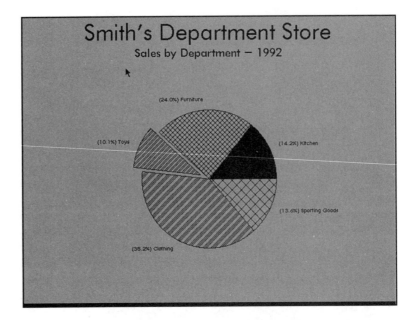

A pie graph.

> ### By the Way . . .
>
> Use a pie graph when you have only a single data series, and want to illustrate the contribution of each individual value to the total.

Blueberry or Apple?

You do have some "pie" options available to you, even though a pie graph may be able to plot only a single Y data range. If you create a B data range and a C data range, then the display of each wedge of the graph is controlled by the value (if any) that you place in the corresponding cell of the B and C ranges:

☛ To display a wedge in a particular color (color graphs) or hatch pattern (black-and-white graphs), enter a value from 1 to 14 in the corresponding cell in the B data range. Each value from 1 to 14 corresponds to a particular color (which depends on your monitor) and a particular hatch pattern (generated by 1-2-3).

☛ To "explode" a wedge, displaying it slightly offset from the rest of the pie for emphasis, add **100** to the value in the corresponding cell of data range **B**.

☛ To suppress display of the percentage value for a slice, enter **0** in the corresponding cell of data range **C**.

The Least You Need to Know

With seven different graphs to choose from, you're sure to find one that's just your type! When selecting a graph type to use, here's what you need to remember.

☛ A *line graph* plots data series as symbols connected by lines. This graph type is good for illustrating changes over time.

☛ A *bar graph* uses bars of different sizes to represent individual data values. It is well suited for making comparisons between groups.

☛ A *stacked bar graph* is a bar graph with the bars for different groups stacked on top of one another instead of side-by-side. Stacked bar graphs can be used to show the relative contribution of each value to its group total.

continues

continued

☛ The *XY graph* is the only graph type that plots values instead of categories on the X axis. It is suited for showing correlations between sets of numerical data.

☛ The *HLCO*, or *high-low-close-open*, is a specialized type of graph for displaying stock market information.

☛ A *mixed graph* combines a bar graph with a line chart. Three data series are plotted as bars, and the other three data series are plotted as lines.

☛ The *pie graph* can plot only a single data series. Individual values are represented as slices of a pie, with the size of each slice proportional to the percent each value contributes to the total.

Chapter 17

Graph Extras—
Optional at No
Extra Cost

In This Chapter

- ☛ Adding titles and a legend to a graph
- ☛ Formatting the graph's axes
- ☛ Enhancing a graph

At the bare minimum, a 1-2-3 graph contains the data range plots and perhaps a set of axes. But that is certainly a "bare" graph. It might be suitable for you to check some data quickly, but it certainly won't do to show the boss! Fortunately, 1-2-3 provides a variety of ways for you to improve your graphs. With a little work, you can turn a basic graph into a work of art, a masterpiece that will surely earn you a promotion and a big raise. Well, maybe not . . . but it can't hurt!

Title, Please

It is probably obvious to you what your graphs mean, but it may not be obvious to other people who are viewing them! Are you showing the firm's annual sales figures, or rainfall in New Guinea? Some well-planned titles can help to identify a graph and the data it is plotting.

A 1-2-3 graph can have two different titles displayed above the graph—these are called the *First* and *Second titles* (the First title is displayed above the Second title, and in larger type). For all graph types except Pie, you can also have a title on the X-axis and one on the Y-axis.

To add or modify graph titles:

1.   From the **Graph** menu, select Options Titles.

2.   Select the title you want to add or modify: First, Second, X-Axis, or Y-Axis.

3.   If necessary, press **Backspace** to delete any existing title, then type in the new title. To use the contents of a worksheet cell for the title, enter \ followed by the cell address.

4.   Press **Enter**.

Release 2.4 does not provide the ability to place a footnote on your graph.

Take a Note

Sometimes the graph titles are just not enough to provide all the necessary information. Fortunately, you can include additional explanatory information in a *footnote* that is displayed in the lower left corner of the graph. The footnote can have one or two lines.

To add or modify the footnote:

1.   From the **Graph** menu, select Options Titles.

2.   Select Note for the first line of the footnote; select Other-Note for the second line of the footnote.

3.   If necessary, press **Backspace** to delete any existing footnote text, then type in the new text. To use the contents of a worksheet cell for the footnote, enter \ followed by the cell address.

4.   Press **Enter**.

Be a Legend—or at Least Create One

Your graph may contain some very important data—but will people know what they are? What do the blue bars mean, and how about the little squares? You need a *legend* to identify each of the data series in your graph.

A graph legend is displayed below the graph. It displays a sample of the symbol, color, or hatch pattern used for each data series, next to an identifying label. Viewers can quickly tell, for example, that the blue bars represent the Eastern Sales Region, the red bars represent the Central Sales Region, and so on.

Legend: A key that identifies a graph's data ranges by color, symbol, or hatch pattern.

To add a legend to your graph:

1. From the **Graph** menu select Options.

2. Select Legend.

3. Select the data range **A–F** for which you want to specify a legend.

4. Enter the legend text; to use the contents of a worksheet cell for the footnote, enter \ followed by the cell address.

5. Press **Enter**.

6. If necessary, repeat steps 2–4 for other data ranges.

7. Select **Quit**.

If your worksheet contains labels in adjacent cells that identify the graph's data ranges, you can create a legend quickly with them:

1. Select **Options Legend Range**.

2. Specify the range containing the labels, either by entering the range address or by using POINT mode.

3. Press **Enter**, then select **Quit**.

1-2-3 uses the first entry in the range as the legend for the A data range, the second entry for the B data range, and so on.

Formatting the Graph's Axes

When 1-2-3 creates a graph, it applies certain default formatting rules to the axes. These apply to the Y-axis for all graph types (except pie, of course); they apply to the X-axis only for XY graphs:

- Values on the axis are displayed in the *General number format* (this is the same General format as can be applied to worksheet cells, as covered in Chapter 12).

- The *axis scale* (the maximum and minimum value on the axis) is calculated on the basis of the range of data being plotted. (For some graph types, the minimum axis value is zero.)

Axis scale: The maximum and minimum values displayed on a graph's axis.

Many aspects of the Y-axis formatting can be changed if the defaults do not suit you. When you're working with an XY graph, which plots values on the X-axis as well as on the Y-axis, you can change them for the X-axis as well. Simply follow the instructions that follow, substituting the X-scale menu command for the Y-scale menu command as needed.

To change the format used for axis numbers:

1. From the Graph menu select **Options Scale Y-Scale Format**.

2. The next menu displays the format choices. These are the same numeric formats that are used for displaying values in cells (see Chapter 12 for more information). Select the desired format.

3. If necessary, enter the number of decimal points to display.

4. Press **Enter**.

5. Select **Quit** twice to return to the Graph menu.

> ## By the Way . . .
> When plotting dollars-and-cents amounts, consider using **Comma** format instead of Currency format for the Y-axis. Having a dollar sign in front of each axis value can be distracting. If you feel the need to indicate that the numbers represent dollars, you can indicate it in the axis title.

Scaling the Heights

The axis scale selected automatically by 1-2-3 does not always display your data in the best way. For example, if you are plotting values in the range 140,000 to 150,000 on a bar graph, 1-2-3 will scale the Y-axis from 0 to 200,000 automatically. As shown in the figure, the relatively small differences between the bars will not be particularly obvious in the graph.

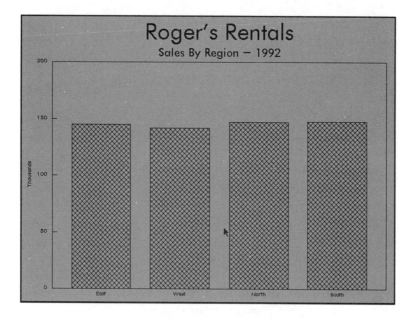

With automatic axis scaling, small differences between large values can be obscured.

Fortunately, 1-2-3 permits you to turn off automatic axis scaling, and set the axis maximum and minimum manually. Here's how:

1. From the **Graph** menu, select Options Scale Y-scale **Manual**.
2. Select Lower.
3. Type in the desired lower-axis scale value, then press **Enter**.
4. Select Upper.
5. Type in the desired upper-axis scale value, then press **Enter**.
6. Select Quit twice to return to the Graph menu.

The figure following shows the same graph with the Y-axis scale set manually to a lower value of 140,000 and an upper value of 150,000. You can see that the differences between the bars are much easier to see now.

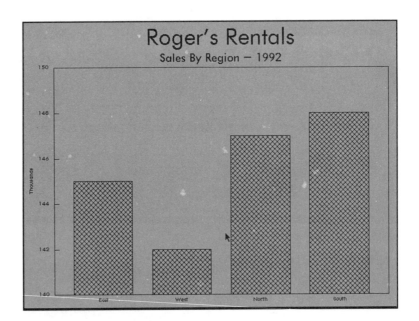

With the Y-axis set manually, the graph gets its message across much better.

My Graph Is Perfect—or Is It?

Once you have created a basic graph in 1-2-3, is that it? Not on your life! The WYSIWYG add-in provides graph editing capabilities; these let you add various elements to a graph to improve its appearance and enhance its effectiveness. For example, you can add lines, arrows, rectangles, and other shapes, and can place text anywhere you want. You can also modify objects you added previously.

To return the Y-axis to automatic scaling, select **O**ptions **S**cale **Y**-scale **A**utomatic from the **Graph** menu.

The Graph Editing Window

To edit a graph you must display it in the *graph editing window*. To do this, a graph must first be displayed in the worksheet (as will be described in Chapter 18). Then,

1. Select :Graph Edit.

2. Move the cell pointer to any cell in the worksheet range where the graph is displayed.

3. Press **Enter**.

When a graph is loaded into the graph editing window, the **Graph Edit** menu is displayed at the top of the screen. You select commands from this menu to edit your graph, or to return to READY mode.

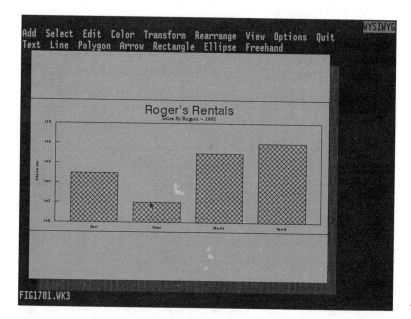

The graph editing window.

Your Selection, Please

Many of the graph editing commands require that you first select an object on the graph to work with. This brings up two questions: what is an "object," and what does "selecting" an object mean?

In READY mode, you can move a graph into the graph editing window by double-clicking on it.

An *object* is a part of the graph, such as an arrow or text you have added. The underlying graphic—that is, the original 1-2-3 graph you're working with—is an object too.

SPEAK LIKE A GEEK

Selection indicator: Small filled squares displayed on selected objects in the graph editing window.

By selecting one or more objects, you are telling the graph editor which item(s) you want to delete, modify, and so on. Selected objects are indicated by *selection indicators*, small filled squares displayed on or around the edges of the object. At any one time, there can be zero, one, or multiple objects selected. In the figure, the rectangle in the upper right corner of the graph is selected.

The selected object (in this figure, the rectangle) has selection indicators displayed on it.

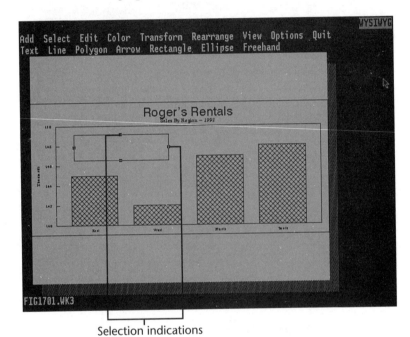

Selection indications

By the Way . . .

In the graph editing window the original 1-2-3 graph is treated as a single object. You cannot select parts of the graph (such as the title or legend) for manipulation. You can only manipulate the graph as a whole.

Here's how to select objects in the graph editing window:

To select...	Do this...
A single object	Click on the object with the mouse, or choose Select One, use the **arrow** keys to move the crosshair cursor to the object, then press **Enter**.
All objects	Choose Select All.
Multiple objects	Choose Select More/Less. Use the **arrow** keys or the mouse to move the crosshair cursor to each object, and press **Spacebar** to select or deselect it. When the desired objects are selected, press **Enter**.
The underlying graph	Choose Select Graph.
Nothing	Choose Select None.

Putting on an Addition

When a graph is displayed in the graph editing window, you can add a variety of objects, such as text, arrows, lines, and rect-angles. These added elements can improve the appearance of the graph, and can also help call the viewer's attention to important points.

To select multiple objects with the mouse, press and hold **Shift** then click on each object.

Cursor on the Move

When you are adding objects in the graph editing window, many opera-tions make use of a small *crosshair cursor* (a thin vertical line crossed by a thin horizontal line) you must move to specify the location and size of the object. You can move the cursor with the mouse (which is easier) or with the keyboard arrow keys. Each time you press an arrow key, the cursor moves by a very small amount. If you press an arrow key repeatedly, the cursor will move by larger amounts. To move the cursor longer distances, you can also press an arrow key and hold it down.

Here are directions for adding objects to the graph:

To add...	Do this...
A line or an arrow	Select Add Line or Add Arrow. Move the cursor to the start of the line or arrow, and click or press **Spacebar**. Move the cursor to the end of the line or arrow, and double-click or press **Enter**.
A rectangle or an ellipse	Select Add Rectangle or Add Ellipse. Move the cursor to where you want the object to start, then press and hold the mouse button or press **Spacebar**. Move the cursor until the outline is the proper size, then release the mouse button or press **Enter**.
Text	Select Add Text. Type in the text (it will appear in the control panel) or, to use the contents of a worksheet cell type \ followed by the cell address. Press **Enter**. The text will appear on the graph at the cursor. Move the cursor to the desired location then click or press **Enter**.
Freehand	Move the cursor to the start location, then press and hold the mouse button or press **Spacebar**. Move the cursor to create the drawing; when finished, release the mouse button or press **Enter**.

Editing the Night Away

The graph window's editing commands are used to modify the appearance, size, and position of graph objects. Use the commands to "fine-tune" the appearance of your graph. There are quite a number of editing commands, only a few of which can be covered here.

You should note that certain editing commands make sense for only certain kinds of objects. For example, it makes sense to change the line style of an arrow object, but not of a text object. Likewise, you can change the font of a text object but not of a rectangle object. 1-2-3 will not prevent you from entering inappropriate editing commands, but they will have no effect.

To force a rectangle into a square, an ellipse into a circle, or a line or arrow to the nearest 45-degree angle, hold **Shift** while drawing the object.

To delete one or more objects:

1. Select the object(s).

2. Choose **Rearrange Delete**.

To move an object:

1. Select the object.

2. Choose **Rearrange Move**.

To delete an object quickly, select it and press **Del**.

3. Use the mouse or the **arrow** keys to move the object to the desired location.

4. Click or press **Enter**.

To change a non-text object's size:

To recover an object that was deleted accidentally, select **Rearrange Restore**. This works only for the most recent deletion.

1. Select the object.

2. Choose Transform Size.

3. Use the **arrow** keys or the mouse to stretch or shrink the outline to the desired size.

4. Click or press **Enter**.

To edit a text object:

1. Select the object.

2. Choose Edit Text.

3. The existing text is displayed in the control panel. Edit it as desired.

Mouse users can move an object quickly by pointing at it and dragging it to the new location. (Remember, *dragging* means to press and hold the left mouse button, move to the new location, then release the button.)

4. Press **Enter**.

To change the font of a text object:

1. Select the object.

2. Choose **Edit Font**.

3. Choose the desired font.

The Least You Need to Know

There are lots of plain, ordinary graphs—then there's the occasional graph that knocks your socks off. Well, maybe I exaggerate a bit, but there are documented cases of graphs that have loosened someone's support hose! If you want your graphs to make a real impression, here's what you need to remember:

- ☛ Use the /Graph Options Titles command to add titles to a graph and its axes, or to add a footnote.

- ☛ A *graph legend* identifies the data plotted in each of the data ranges. To add a legend to a graph, select /Graph Options Legend.

- ☛ To set the upper and lower limits on the Y-axis manually, select (from the **Graph** menu) Options Scale Y-scale Manual. Then select Lower to enter the lower-axis scale value, and select Upper to enter the upper-axis scale value.

- ☛ To specify the numeric display format for the numbers on the Y-axis, select (from the **Graph** menu) Options Scale Y-scale Format.

- ☛ The *graph editing window* is used to add and modify graph objects. To edit a graph, first you have to display it in the worksheet. Double-click on the graph to move it to the graph editing window, then use the various editing commands to enhance it.

Chapter 18
Displaying and Printing Graphs

In This Chapter

- Displaying graphs in the worksheet
- Changing the size and position of graphs
- Printing graphs

A graph that is never displayed is like a painting that is covered by a sheet—what's the point? You may say that some paintings deserve to be kept covered, but surely that's not true of your beautiful graphs! It's when you display graphs as part of your worksheets, and include them in printed reports, that they are really useful. This chapter shows you how.

Don't Hide Your Graphs!

Graphs are meant to be seen, right? And just like members of high society, *where* they're seen is very important! For a graph, being displayed as part of the worksheet, along with the data and other relevant information, is usually the ideal situation. With 1-2-3 (and the help of WYSIWYG), this is easy to do.

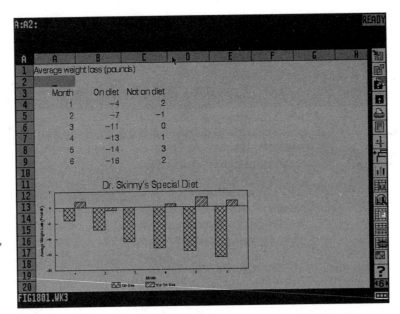

1-2-3 can display a graph in the worksheet along with the data.

A graph can be displayed anywhere in the worksheet, at any size you desire. What's equally important is that graphs can easily be printed as part of your reports (printing is covered later in this chapter). To display a graph in the worksheet:

1. Select :Graph Add.

2. To display the current graph, select Current. To display a named graph, select Named, then press → and ← to highlight the desired graph name, and press **Enter**.

3. 1-2-3 prompts you for the worksheet range where the graph should be displayed. Specify the range by typing in a range address (or by using POINT mode), then press **Enter**.

4. Select Quit to return to READY mode.

Don't remember what the current graph is? Press **F10** in READY mode to view it.

When you add a graph to the worksheet, it is sized automatically to fit the specified range. If the range size changes because rows or columns have been inserted or deleted, the graph is resized to fit the new dimensions.

If you plan to add a graph to the worksheet later, but the graph isn't ready yet, use the :Graph Add Blank command to add an empty *placeholder* to pinch-hit for the graph. Later use the :Graph Settings Graph command to replace the placeholder with the graph.

Graph Be Gone!

Tired of looking at that graph? You can remove a graph from the worksheet as follows:

1. Select :Graph Remove.

2. Move the cell pointer to any cell in the range of the graph you want to remove. (Or press **F3** to see a list of all graphs that are displayed in the worksheet.) Use → and ← to highlight the name of the graph to remove.

3. Press **Enter**.

The :Graph Remove command simply "undisplays" a graph. The graph remains defined—and can be viewed with the /Graph Name Use command, or redisplayed in the worksheet with :Graph Add.

Want a full-screen view of a displayed graph? Move the cell pointer to any cell in the graph range, select :**G**raph **Z**oom, and press **Enter**.

If you add the current graph to the worksheet, and then use the /**G**raph commands to define another graph, the worksheet display will change to reflect the newly-defined graph. For a "permanent" display, you must assign a name to the graph (with /**G**raph **N**ame **Cr**e-ate), then add the graph to the worksheet by name.

By the Way . . .
You can display a graph in a range that contains worksheet data. The data is not affected, but is merely hidden from view while the graph is displayed.

Instead of removing a graph, you may wish simply to hide it temporarily. A hidden graph is displayed as a gray rectangle, and can be unhidden at any time. To hide or unhide a graph:

It's easy to tell when the cell pointer is within a graph range, because the top line of the control panel will display **{Graph GRAPHNAME}** when it is.

1. Select :Graph Settings Display.

2. Select No to hide a graph, or select Yes to unhide a graph.

3. Move the cell pointer to any cell in the range of the graph that you want hidden or displayed. Or, press **F3** to see a list of all graphs that are displayed in the worksheet. Use → and ← to highlight the name of the graph.

4. Press **Enter**.

By the Way . . .

Hiding graphs may improve the speed of 1-2-3, because that way it does not have to redraw the graphs every time the screen is scrolled.

Graph Go Elsewhere

As you polish the appearance of your worksheet, you may find that a displayed graph's location needs to be changed. Here's how to move a graph:

1. Select :Graph Move.

2. Move the cell pointer to any cell in the range of the graph you want to move.

3. Press **Enter**.

4. Move the cell pointer to the cell where you want the top left corner of the graph placed.

5. Press **Enter**.

When you use the :Graph Move command, there is no change in the graph's size or the other aspects of its appearance.

The Incredible Shrinking (or Expanding) Graph

Graph too small? Or maybe it's too big. In either case, there's no problem. You can change the size of a displayed graph quickly, as follows:

1. Select :**Graph Settings Range**.

2. Move the cell pointer to any cell in the range of the graph you want to resize. (Or press **F3** to see a list of all graphs that are displayed in the worksheet.) Use → and ← to highlight the name of the graph to resize.

3. Press **Enter**. 1-2-3 highlights the graph's current display range, and switches to POINT mode. The upper left corner of the range is anchored, and the lower right corner is free.

4. Use the **arrow** keys to expand or contract the graph range. If necessary, press . one or more times to move the free cell to other corners of the range.

5. When the range is the desired size, press **Enter**.

Graph, You're Being Replaced

A displayed graph can be replaced with any other worksheet graph, or with a blank placeholder. The new graph will have the same size and position as the graph it replaces. Here are the steps to follow:

1. Select :**Graph Settings Graph**.

2. Move the cell pointer to any cell in the range of the graph you want to replace. (Or press **F3** to see a list of all graphs that are displayed in the worksheet.) Use → and ← to highlight the name of the graph to replace.

3. Press **Enter**.

4. From the menu, select the item you want the graph replaced with: **Current** for the current graph, **Blank** for a blank place-holder, or **Named** for a named graph. If you select Named, 1-2-3 displays a list of existing named graphs. Use the ← and → keys to highlight the desired name, then press **Enter**.

5. Select **Quit**.

By the Way . . .

Replacing a graph affects only the underlying graphic (the original 1-2-3 graph). The procedure will not remove any enhancements that were made with the **:G**raph **E**dit commands.

Keeping Up to Date

1-2-3 normally updates all displayed graphs each time the worksheet is recalculated (see Chapter 9 for information on worksheet recalculation). *Update* means that all graphs are changed to reflect any changes in the worksheet data. Automatic graph updating is usually fine, since it ensures that all graphs in the worksheet are accurate. With large, complicated worksheets that contain a number of graphs, however, you may want to turn automatic updating off to improve program speed. Here's how:

1. Select **:G**raph **S**ettings **S**ync.

2. Select **No** to disable automatic updating, or select **Yes** to enable it.

3. Move the cell pointer to any cell in the range of the graph whose update setting you want to change. (Or press **F3** to see a list of all graphs that are displayed in the worksheet.) Use → and ← to highlight the name of the graph.

4. Press **Enter**.

To update all graphs in the worksheet manually, select **:G**raph **C**ompute.

> **By the Way . . .**
> Setting worksheet recalculation to **Manual** (with the /Worksheet Global Recalculation Manual command) does not disable automatic updating of displayed graphs.

Printing Graphs

Printing graphs is very easy. In fact, it's no different from printing regular worksheet data. All you do is specify a print range that includes the graph.

Chapter 14 covers worksheet printing, and you should look there for details. Here are the basic steps for printing a worksheet range that includes a graph.

1. Select **:Print** to display the Print menu and the Print Settings dialog box.

2. Look at the **Print range(s)** entry in the Print Settings dialog box. If there is an existing print range, select **Range Clear** to delete it.

3. Select **Range Set**.

4. Specify the range to print by typing in a range address or range name (or by using POINT mode), then press **Enter**. Be sure the range includes the entire extent of the graph(s) you want printed.

5. Select **Go**. 1-2-3 will begin printing, and will display **WAIT** in the mode indicator while the print job is in progress. When the job is complete, you will return to READY mode.

Avoiding Splits

Depending on the size of your graph, the size of the print range, and other print settings, a graph may happen to fall on a *page break* (the split between one printed page and the next). When this happens, the graph will be printed split between two pages—clearly not acceptable!

To print just a graph, specify a print range that includes only the graph.

After setting your print range, you should use the :Print Preview command to preview your print job to ensure that no graphs are split between pages. (See Chapter 14 for details on :Print Preview.) If everything seems OK, you can go ahead and print. If a graph is split, however, what can you do?

The first step is to return to READY mode and look at the worksheet. Remember that 1-2-3 displays dashed vertical and horizontal lines in the worksheet, indicating the locations of page breaks. If a graph overlaps a page break by only one or two rows or columns, you may be able to adjust the graph's size or location to solve the problem.

If the problem is more serious, you can insert one or more page breaks. In addition to the actual split between pages, the term *page break* refers to a command that tells 1-2-3 to start printing on a new page at a particular worksheet row or column. By inserting a page break just before a graph, you can prevent it from being split between two pages.

There are two types of page break commands. A *Row page break* specifies that a new page is to start at the specified row, and a *Column page break* specifies that a new page is to start at the specified column. Here's how to add and remove page breaks:

1. Place the cell pointer in the first row or column you want on a new page.

2. Select :Worksheet Page.

3. Select Row or Column.

4. Select Quit.

By the Way . . .

Remember, 1-2-3 prints multiple-page jobs top-to-bottom, then in left-to-right order.

To delete a page break:

1. Move the cell pointer to the row or column containing the page break.

2. Select **:Worksheet Page Delete**.

3. Select **Quit**.

In READY mode, when the cell pointer is in a row or column that contains a page break, {MPage} is displayed in the control panel.

The Least You Need to Know

Displaying graphs as part of the worksheet, and including them in printouts, is one of my favorite 1-2-3 features. The only problem is that my boss knows about it too, so I have no excuse for producing anything less than great-looking worksheets and reports! To be sure your boss doesn't know more than you do, remember these points:

- ☛ You can display the current graph or a named graph anywhere in the worksheet, at any size you want. To do so, use the **:Graph Add** command.

- ☛ Once a graph is displayed in the worksheet, you can move it to another location (with the **:Graph Move** command), change its size (with the **:Graph Settings Range** command), or remove it completely (with the **:Graph Remove** command).

- ☛ To print a graph, all you need to do is include the graph in the print range when you use the **:Print** command. You can print a graph by itself, or in combination with worksheet data.

- ☛ Use the **:Print Preview** command to check the appearance of your report before you actually print it. If a graph is split across a page break, you can use **:Worksheet Page** to move the page break so the graph is printed on one page.

This page unintentionally left blank.

Part V
Database Delights

1-2-3 isn't all numbers and graphs. You can also use a worksheet to maintain a database, a collection of similarly formatted information such as a name and address list or a parts inventory. This section covers the tasks of creating a database, keeping the information sorted in the desired order, and locating specific information.

Chapter 19

Databases From Step One

In This Chapter

- ☞ What is a database?
- ☞ Starting a database
- ☞ Entering new information
- ☞ Sorting a database

A 1-2-3 *database* is a flexible method for storing and manipulating certain kinds of information. You could, for example, keep track of all your heavy metal CD's, or maintain a list of all "B-grade" horror flicks you have seen. In extreme circumstances, you could even do something useful, like maintaining your firm's employee records or mailing list! For many kinds of information, using a database is easier and more flexible than keeping the information in some other worksheet format. This chapter gets you started with 1-2-3 databases.

Database, Will You Be Mine?

The term "database" may sound a bit technical, but there's nothing at all complicated about it. I'll bet you are already using at least one database. If you keep an address book or maintain a register in your checkbook, then I win my bet!

Database: A collection of data items that all have the same structure, but each contain different information.

Record: One complete database entry.

Field: An item of information contained in each database record.

Field names: Unique names that identify the fields in a database table.

A database is nothing more than a method of storing information—in which each individual entry, called a *record*, has the same structure. In a checkbook register, for example, each entry has the same five parts: "Check number," "date," "payee," "amount," and "category." Each entry in the register will contain different information, of course, but they all have the same five parts—the same structure.

When working with databases, there is some terminology you need to understand. A *record* is one complete database entry. In the checkbook register example, the information about each check comprises one record. A field is an item of information contained in each record. In our example there are five fields: "Check number," "date," "payee," "amount," and "category."

Databases and Worksheets

How do databases relate to 1-2-3 worksheets? You may have already realized that the structure of a database fits perfectly into the row-and-column structure of a worksheet. Each database field gets its own column, and each database record gets its own row. The top row of a 1-2-3 database contains *field names* (unique names that identify the database fields).

A rectangular region in a single worksheet that contains data organized in this fashion is called a *database table*. A 1-2-3 database can contain multiple database tables, located in one or more worksheets. I will limit discussion, however, to *single-table databases* (the kind you will use most often). The following figure shows a 1-2-3 database table.

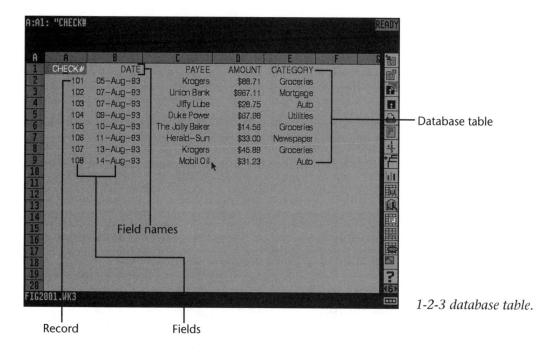

1-2-3 database table.

What kind of data can you keep in a database table? There are no restrictions; any kind of data that can be put in a worksheet can be used in a database table. The only rule you should follow (from record to record) is to be sure that all of the entries in each field are the same *data type*—value or label. 1-2-3 will not prevent you from entering inconsistent data types in a field, but you may get incorrect results during certain database operations like searching and sorting.

Put It to Work

In a mailing-list database, enter ZIP codes as *labels*. If you enter them as values, you will not be able to display or print the leading zero in codes such as 07211. They will still sort properly as labels.

Starting a Database

The first step in creating a database table is to do a little planning. Careful planning at this stage will make many database operations easier and less prone to error. You need to consider the following points:

☞ What fields will the database table contain? For example, does your checkbook register need a "Tax deduction" field?

☞ What will the field names be? The names should be descriptive of the information stored in the field, but they should also be as short as is practical. For example, instead of "Check number" you could use "Check#" or "num".

☞ How will the fields be organized? In other words, what will the left-to-right order of fields be in the database table?

By the Way . . .

If your database table includes a "Date" field, be sure to *enter dates as serial numbers,* and not simply as labels that look like dates. Otherwise you will not be able to sort the database table by date. Format that entire column with the Automatic format command (/**R**ange **F**ormat **O**ther **A**utomatic). Then, dates you enter in a standard date format (for example, **12-Sep-93**) will be converted automatically to the corresponding date serial number, and displayed in date format.

Once these questions have been answered, you are ready to start your database table. The procedure is actually quite simple:

1. Find a region of the worksheet that has enough room to hold the database table, including future expansion.

2. Enter the field names in the first row of the database table.

3. Enter the data for the first record in the second row of the table.

4. Enter data for additional records in the third and subsequent rows.

5. If desired, change formatting, column widths, and label alignment to best display the data.

That's all there is to it! A database table can contain as many records as you like, up to the maximum imposed by the number of rows in a worksheet (8,192). A database table cannot contain any blank rows—although individual records can contain one or more blank fields, as long as at least one field contains data. To add new records to the database table, move to the first blank row at the end of the table, and start entering data.

> ## By the Way . . .
>
> Do not include a *separator row* between the field names and the first record of the database. If you want to separate the field names from the data visually, use the **:Format Lines Bottom** command to place a border under the field names.

What Sort Are You?

There will probably be times when you want the records in your database table *sorted* in a particular order. You could sort your checkbook database by date or by check number, for example, or a mailing list database could be sorted in ZIP code order. 1-2-3 can sort a database on the basis of the contents of one or more database fields. A field that is used to order records in a sort is called a *sort key*.

Sort key: A database field used to order records when the database is sorted.

You always specify one field to be the *primary sort key* when sorting a database. You can also specify another field as the *secondary sort key*; the secondary sort key is used to order the records when there is a tie in the primary sort key. A sort can be done in either ascending or descending order. Ascending order sorts labels in alphabetical order (A–Z), and numbers smallest to largest; descending order uses reverse alphabetical order (Z–A), and numbers largest to smallest.

If the field names seem to have disappeared after you sort the database, it is probably because you included them in the sort range. If the Undo feature is enabled, you can press **Alt+F4** to restore the database table to its original order.

To sort a database table quickly on a single key, position the cell pointer in the column containing the desired sort field, and click on the **Ascending sort** or **Descending sort** SmartIcon: or

Check the settings in the QuickSort dialog box, then click on **OK**.

Here's how to sort the records in a database table:

1. Select /Data Sort Data-range.

2. Type in a range address or range name (or use POINT mode) to specify the range containing all of the database table's records (but *not* the field names).

3. Press **Enter**.

4. Select **Primary-key**.

5. Move the cell pointer to any cell in the column that contains the field you want to use as the primary sort key, then press **Enter**.

6. Press **A** for an ascending sort or **D** for a descending sort, then press **Enter**.

7. If you want to use a secondary sort key, select **Secondary-key**, then repeat steps 5 and 6 to specify the secondary sort's key field and sort order.

8. Select **Go** to sort the records.

The next two figures show a database before and after sorting on the CATEGORY field.

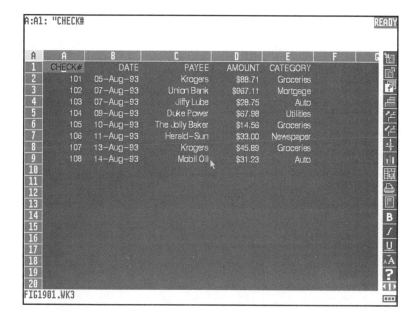

The database before being sorted.

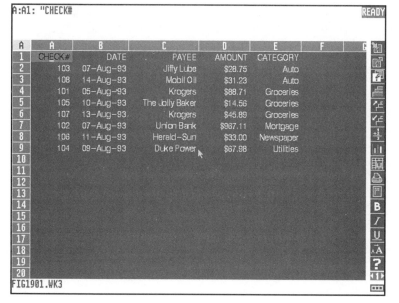

The database after being sorted in ascending order with CATEGORY as the primary sort key.

You can sort a database table as many times and as many ways as you like. The sorting procedure has no effect on the data in the records; it only changes the order of the records in the table. If you add new records to a sorted database, you must re-sort the database if you want all the records to be in order.

The Least You Need to Know

Now you are ready to "get on base" with your data by using 1-2-3's database capabilities. As you run toward home plate, don't forget the basics:

☞ A *database* is a data storage format where each item of information, called a *record*, has the same structure (contains the same *fields*). In a worksheet, a database table is stored with each row corresponding to a record and each column corresponding to a field.

☞ Each field in a database table must be identified by a unique name. The *field names* are placed in the top row of the database table.

☞ A database table can contain both values and labels. The only restriction is that each field (or column) should contain either values or labels, and not a mixture of both.

☞ You use the /**D**ata **S**ort command to sort the records in a database table. You can order the records on the basis of the data in one or more fields (called *sort keys*), and can specify either ascending or descending order.

Chapter 20

Data, Where Are You?

In This Chapter

- ☞ Setting up your criteria range
- ☞ Finding matching records
- ☞ Extracting matching records
- ☞ Deleting matching records

Having your data neatly organized in a 1-2-3 database table is great—but what do you do if you want to locate some specific information? You would think that a computer should make this sort of task simple, and that's true. 1-2-3 offers a number of different methods for finding and manipulating specific information in a database table.

The Search Is On!

Using a 1-2-3 worksheet to store database information is fine, but what happens when you need to find and retrieve some specific information? Do you have to look through the database's records manually, one at a time, until you find what you need? No way!

1-2-3 has several different tools that let you locate specific information in a database and work with it. These tools are covered later in the chapter. Whichever tool you use, however, you need some way to tell 1-2-3 what you're looking for. Let's look at that first.

Holy Criteria!

When you are looking for specific records in a database, you need some way to tell 1-2-3 which records will be considered a "match," and which will not. For example:

- ☛ In a mailing list database, match all records where the STATE field contains "NY."

- ☛ In a sales database, match all records where the TOTAL field is greater than 1000.

- ☛ In a checkbook-register database, match all records where the PAYEE field contains "Cash" and the AMOUNT field is greater than or equal to 100.

All of the above are examples of *criteria*—information or rules that tell 1-2-3 which records you're looking for. When you are working with a database table, you specify the criteria in a *criteria range*. As you have probably guessed, a criteria range is a section of the worksheet where you place the search criteria.

Criteria: A set of rules, or patterns, that specifies which records in a database table to match. (Note: "criteria" is plural; the singular is "criterion.")

Criteria range: A worksheet range in which you enter search criteria for finding records in a database table.

A criteria range contains as many columns as the database table has fields. It will usually have two rows, and sometimes will have more. The first row contains an exact copy of the database table's field names, one per column. Beneath each field name, you place the criterion that applies to that field. To find all the records in a mailing-list database where the STATE field contains "CA," for example, you would enter **CA** directly below the **STATE** field name in the criteria range.

The following sections describe the various kinds of criteria you can use in your criteria range. I will use the check-register database table that I introduced in the previous chapter as a source of examples.

Exactly So

Exact matches are the easiest. You simply enter the value or label that you want to find under the corresponding field name. For example, to find records for checks made out to "Cash," the criteria range would be as follows:

Check#	Date	Payee	Amount	Category
		Cash		

Similarly, to search for all records where "Amount" is equal to 100:

Check#	Date	Payee	Amount	Category
			100	

Getting Wild

When you are entering a criterion for a label field, you can use *wild card characters* to help find groups of records. In criteria, the * wild card character represents any group of zero or more characters, and the ? wild card character represents any single character. You could, therefore, find any "Category" that starts with "House" (such as "House repairs" or "House insurance") with this criterion:

Check#	Date	Payee	Amount	Category
				House*

And you could find a check written to Tom Andersen or Tom Anderson as follows:

Check#	Date	Payee	Amount	Category
		Tom Anders?n		

Wild card characters:
When entering criteria for /**Data F**ind operations, ***** and **?** are wild card characters that match any one character (**?**), or any group of zero or more characters (*****).

Not!

The ~ character, called a *tilde*, means "anything but." By preceding a criterion with this character, you instruct 1-2-3 to match anything *except* the specified criterion. The following criteria range would match all records except those where the CATEGORY field contains "Entertainment."

Check#	Date	Payee	Amount	Category
				~Entertainment

In-Between

When searching for a value, is there some way to find anything that falls within a certain range? You bet! To do so, you will need to use some special operators. These are called the *relational operators* because they express certain relationships between values. They are listed, with their meanings, in this table.

Operator	Meaning (relationship)
<>	Not equal to
>	Greater than
<	Less than
<=	Less than or equal to
>=	Greater than or equal to

> **By the Way . . .**
>
> When entering criteria that use the "less than" relational operator (<), be sure to enter the label prefix character ' first. Otherwise, when you press <, 1-2-3 will display the menu—because < is 1-2-3's "alternative" menu key, and works the same as /.

So, to find all records where "Amount" is greater than 100, you would use the following criteria range:

Check#	Date	Payee	Amount	Category
			>100	

Likewise, to search for all records with "Check#" less than or equal to 200:

Check#	Date	Payee	Amount	Category
<=200				

AND, OR (But No Buts)

When you're working with a database, you will sometimes need to locate records based on two or more criteria. For example, you might want to locate checks that were written to Union Bank for amounts greater than $100.00. As another example, you might want to find all checks written for the categories "Auto" and "Entertainment."

In both of these examples there are two search criteria. In the first example the search criteria are: "Payee" equals "Union Bank," and "Amount" is greater than 100. In other words, both criteria have to be true for a record to be considered a match. In the second example, there are also two criteria: "Category" equals "Auto" or "Category" equals "Entertainment." A record is considered a match if either one of the criteria is met.

Notice the difference here. In the first example, *both* criteria must be true for there to be a match; in the second example, only one of the two criteria must be true. This illustrates the fact that when searching a database on two criteria, there are two ways in which the two criteria can be "combined" to determine whether a given record is a match or not. You combine multiple criteria either by placing the individual criteria in specific locations in the criteria range, or by using the #AND# and #OR# operators. These two methods of combining criteria work as follows:

- ☞ **OR:** matches if either one of the criteria are met. You specify OR by typing #OR# between two criteria in a worksheet cell in the criteria range, or by placing the criteria on different rows in the criteria range.

- ☞ **AND:** matches only if both criteria are met. You specify AND by typing #AND# between two criteria in a worksheet cell in the criteria range, or by placing the criteria in different columns on the same row in the criteria range.

By the Way . . .

The #OR# operator also results in a match if both criteria are met. This makes no sense in our example—a record can't have *both* "Auto" and "Entertainment" in the CATEGORY field. In other situations, however, it can be useful.

OR operator: When searching a database on two criteria, the OR operator specifies that a record will be considered a match if either one (or both) of the criteria are met.

AND operator: When searching a database on two criteria, the AND operator specifies that a record will be considered a match only if both of the criteria are met.

To use two criteria in your database searches, combine them using AND and OR, as shown in the following examples. In these examples, I have listed only those field names that have criteria entered under them. Remember that normally your criteria range will include *all* the field names.

To find checks that were written to Union Bank for amounts greater than $100.00:

Payee	Amount
Union Bank	>100

To find checks written for amounts between $500 and $1000:

Amount

+D2>=500#AND#D2<=1000

You may be wondering why there are two references to cell D2 in this criterion. It's to tell 1-2-3 where to find the data to "plug into" the criterion. In this example, the AMOUNT field is in column D, and the first record is in row 2. In your database tables the required cell reference will probably be different. These cell references are necessary in criteria that use the #AND# or the #OR# operators.

To find checks with check numbers below 200 or above 500, you could use either of the following two criteria ranges. The first example uses the #OR# operator to specify the OR relationship between the two criteria; the second example uses position (the "Check#" field is in column A, and the first record is in row 2):

Check#

+A2<200#OR#A2>500

Check#

<200

>500

TECHNO NERD TEACHES

A *logical formula* is a formula that evaluates some condition and determines whether it is true or not. For example, +**C5=100** is a logical formula, asking the question, "Is the value in cell C5 equal to 100?" Because computers work with numbers, it has become conventional to represent "False" by the value 0, and "True" by a non-zero value (usually 1). If you enter this formula in a worksheet cell, it will display either 0 or 1, depending on the value in cell C5.

By the Way . . .

A cell in a criteria range containing a logical formula will display either 0 or 1, depending on whether the first record in the database table meets the specified criteria. It's usually better to display the criteria formula instead of the result (0 or 1); this way it's easier to tell what the criteria are asking. To do so, use the /**Range Format** command to assign the **Text** format to the cell(s).

How About a Date?

If you want to perform a search based on dates, you will be wise to store dates in your database table as date serial numbers. This enables you to perform searches for ranges of dates, dates later than a certain date, and so on. Because you will be searching on the basis of date serial numbers, your criteria must use serial numbers as well. They are most easily obtained using the **@Date** function. For example, to find all checks written after January 1, 1993 (the "Date" field is in column B):

Date

+B2>@DATE(93,1,1)

Data Query Operations

Once you have set up your criteria range, as described in the first part of this chapter, you are ready to locate information in your database table. There are several different "search" operations, all accessed via the /Data Query command. Which one you use depends on your specific needs.

Lost and Found

To locate matching records in your database table, use the /Data Query Find command. 1-2-3 will highlight each matching record; you can view it, edit it, and so on. Here are the steps to follow.

1.   Set up the desired criteria in a criteria range.

2.   Select /Data Query Input.

3.   Specify the data table range, including the row of field names, by typing in a range address or range name (or by using POINT mode), then press **Enter**.

4.   Select Criteria.

5.   Specify the criteria range, then press **Enter**.

6.   Select Find. 1-2-3 highlights the first record in the database table that meets the criteria. You can then use the following keys to view and modify the data.

↓, ↑	Move the highlight to the next or previous matching record.
Home, End	Move the highlight to the first or last matching record in the table.
←, →	Move the cursor between fields in the high-lighted record.
F2	Edit the current field; press **Enter** when done.
F7	Return to READY mode.
Esc	End the Find operation and return to the /Data Query menu.

A Painless Extraction

To copy matching records to another part of the worksheet, use the /Data Query Extract command. This is useful if you want to print the matching records, or use them in a graph. In the figure, the range A13..E16 contains records with CATEGORY="Groceries" extracted from the database table in range A1..E9. Here's how to perform an extraction:

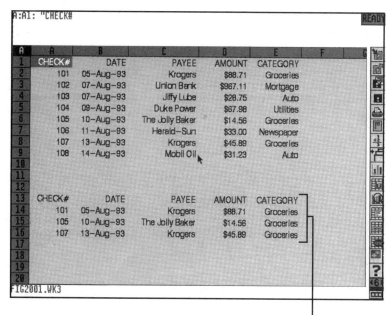

The records in the range A13..E16 were extracted from the database table with the /Data Query Extract command.

Extracted range

1. Copy the database table's field names to a blank area of the worksheet. The copied records will be placed below the field names.

2. Set up the desired criteria in a criteria range.

3. Select /Data Query Input.

4. Specify the data table range, including the row of field names, by typing in a range address or range name (or by using POINT mode), then press **Enter**.

5. Select **Output**.

6. Specify the one-row range containing the copied field names, then press **Enter**.

7. Select **Criteria**.

8. Specify the criteria range, then press **Enter**.

9. Select **Extract**. 1-2-3 copies all matching records to the output range.

10. Select **Quit** to return to READY mode.

When you perform an extract operation, the original database table is not changed in any way.

Data, You're History!

To delete matching records from a database table, use the /Data Query Delete command.

Use /**File S**ave to save your worksheet before performing a /**Data Q**uery **D**elete operation. This way you can get your original data back if you make a mistake, even if Undo is not enabled!

1. Set up the desired criteria in a criteria range.

2. Select /Data Query Input.

3. Specify the data table range, including the row of field names, by typing in a range address or range name (or by using POINT mode), then press **Enter**.

4. Select **Criteria**.

5. Specify the criteria range, then press **Enter**.

6. Select **Del**; when asked for confirmation, select **Del** again. 1-2-3 deletes all matching records from the database table, and moves remaining records up to fill the deleted rows.

The Least You Need to Know

The *criteria range* contains information that 1-2-3 uses to determine which database records will be considered a "match" and which will not.

☞ The first row of the criteria range contains a copy of the database table's field names. Below the field names you place specific selection criteria.

☞ When setting up a criteria range that uses two or more criteria, you indicate the AND relationship by placing the criteria on the same row of the criteria range, or by using the #AND# operator. You indicate the OR relationship by placing the criteria on different rows of the criteria range, or by using the #OR# operator.

☞ Once your criteria have been set up, you use /**Data Query F**ind to locate matching records, /**Data Query E**xtract to copy matching records to another location, and /**Data Query D**elete to erase matching records.

This page unintentionally left blank.

Appendix A
Installing 1-2-3

If you're lucky, 1-2-3 has already been installed on your computer and is ready to go. If you aren't and it's not, you may have to do it yourself. Don't panic! It's really not all that difficult. Lotus provides a very friendly and easy-to-use installation program that does most of the work for you. Once the installation program is running, all you need do is answer a few relatively simple questions on-screen, and swap some diskettes in and out of the drive. This appendix walks you through the process step-by-step.

Before you start the installation process, you need to gather a little bit of information. You may know these things already, or you may have to go and ask someone.

- ☞ You need to know the *letters of your computer's diskette drives*. If there's only a single diskette drive, it is almost sure to be *A:*, so you're all set. If there are two drives they will be called A: and B:, but which is which? Here's a hint: When you first turn on your computer, one of the two drives will be activated briefly, even if there's no diskette in it. You can tell by the little light on the front of the drive that comes on. This is drive A:, the other one is drive B:.

- ☞ You need to know the *letter of the hard disk you are installing 1-2-3 on.* This is almost always *C:*.

- ☞ You need to know the *manufacturer and the model name/number of your printer.*

The procedure for installing release 2.4 of 1-2-3 is almost identical to that for release 3.4. You start the Install program the same way, make screen selections the same way, and so on. Some of the steps occur in a different order (for example, specifying which programs to install is done sooner), but otherwise the descriptions that follow will serve you well. The only major difference is that release 2.4 asks you to specify both a Text printer and a Graphics printer. This is confusing until you realize that these are one and the same printer; you should specify the make and model of your printer for both.

Once you have this information, you're ready to start. To begin the installation process, you must have the DOS prompt, which usually looks like **C:>** or **C:\>**, displayed on your screen. Then:

1. Place the 1-2-3 diskette labeled **Disk 1 (Install)** into your diskette drive.

2. Type the letter of the diskette drive (**A** or **B**) followed by a colon (**a :**), then press **Enter**. The DOS prompt will change to **A:>** or **A:\>** (or if you're using drive B:, to B:> or B:\>).

3. Type **INSTALL** and press **Enter**. The diskette will whirr for a moment, and the installation program will display its opening screen, as shown in the following figure.

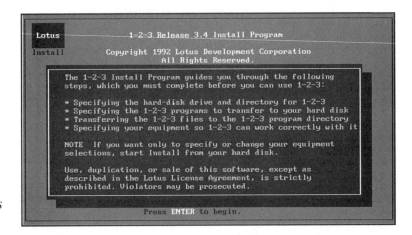

The Install program's opening screen.

If you've gotten this far, congratulations! You've started the Install program and are on your way. Read the information on the screen, if you like, then press **Enter**.

If this is the first time 1-2-3 has been installed from this set of diskettes, the Install program will next ask you to enter your name and the name of your organization. Type in the information, and confirm it by pressing **Enter**. If 1-2-3 has been installed previously from your diskettes, this step will be skipped.

The next steps let you specify the disk and directory where you want 1-2-3 installed, and which programs to copy:

1. The next screen asks you for the letter of the hard drive on which 1-2-3 is to be installed. If you're using drive C:, press **Enter**. To install to a different drive, type the drive letter (with no following colon), then press **Enter**.

2. The next screen asks for the name of the directory where 1-2-3 and add-ins should be installed. Unless you have a specific reason to use another directory, press **Enter** to accept the default directory **C:\123R34**, then press **Enter** again to accept the default **C:\123R34\ADDINS** as the 1-2-3 add-in directory.

3. On the next screen (shown in the following figure), you can specify which programs should be installed. Selected programs are marked with a checkmark. You can move the highlight with the ↑ and ↓ keys, and view a description of the highlighted program in the box. The main program ("1-2-3 Release 3.4") is required; the others are optional. If you are in doubt, accept the default program selections by pressing **Enter**. You can always install the other programs later.

On this screen you select which programs to install.

4. The next screen lets you select which add-in programs are loaded automatically each time you start 1-2-3. Use the ↑ and ↓ keys to move the highlight, and press the **Spacebar** to toggle the highlighted add-in between selected (checked) and unselected. Unless

you have a specific reason to load one or more of these add-ins automatically, press **Enter** to accept the default of none automatically loaded. (Again, you can specify auto-loading of add-ins later.)

The Install program will now start transferring files from the diskettes to your hard disk. This will take a few minutes, and you will be prompted to insert other diskettes in the drive as needed. When the transfer is completed (which may not require all the diskettes, depending on the installation options you selected), a screen will be displayed, explaining that the next steps are for you to specify the equipment you will use with 1-2-3. After reading this screen, press **Enter** to continue.

1. The next screen displays the name of the video display system that 1-2-3 has detected on your computer. Press **Enter**.

2. On the next screen, you'll see a list of all the video display systems that 1-2-3 supports; 1-2-3 highlights the system it detected. Unless you are SURE that you have a different video system, press **Enter** to accept this setting.

3. Depending on the video system you selected, the Install program may next display a screen on which you select the video display mode to use (number of screen columns, use of color, and so on). For some video systems, this step is skipped. Select the desired display mode with the ↑ and ↓ keys, then press **Enter**.

4. The next screen asks if you will be using a printer with 1-2-3. If not, select **No**, press **Enter**, and go to step 8. Otherwise select **Yes**, press **Enter**, and continue.

5. On the next screen, use the ↑ and ↓ keys to highlight the name of your printer manufacturer, and press **Enter**.

6. Next, use the ↑ and ↓ keys to highlight the model name/number of your printer, and press **Enter**.

7. If you're lucky enough to have another printer, select **Yes** on the next screen, and then repeat steps 5 and 6. Otherwise, select No.

8. On the next screen, press **Enter** to accept the default DCF file name **123.DCF**.

You're making great progress, and are almost finished. There's one more step—generating the fonts that 1-2-3 uses for screen display and printing. Press **Enter** to go on.

On the next screen you are given a choice of three font sets: Basic, Medium, or Extended. If you are in doubt as to which one to choose, I suggest **Medium**.

If the Install program asks you **Generate Fonts Now?**, select **Yes**. 1-2-3 will generate its fonts, displaying progress on the screen. If you selected either the Medium of Extended font set, this process will take a while, so you may want to go get a cup of coffee!

When font generation is complete, press any key to exit the Install program and return to the DOS prompt. Congratulations! You are finished. You can now start 1-2-3 (as explained in Chapter 2).

This page unintentionally left blank.

Appendix B
Lotus 1-2-3 @Functions

This appendix will list the Lotus 1-2-3 @functions and a description of each. @Functions are built-in 1-2-3 formulas that calculate automatically. See Chapter 10 of this book for more information on how to use @functions.

@@(*location*)
> Gets the contents of the cell in the location specified

@ABS(*x*)
> Calculates the absolute value of x

@ACOS(*x*)
> Calculates the arc cosine of x

@ASIN(*x*)
> Calculates the arc sine of x

@ATAN(*x*)
> Calculates the arc tangent of x

@ATAN2(*x*)
> Calculates the arc tangent using the tangent *y/x* of an angle

@AVG(*list*)
> Calculates the average of a list of values

@CELL(*attribute, location*)
> Returns information about a cell

@CELLPOINTER(*attribute*)
> Returns information about the current cell

@CHAR(*x*)
> Returns the character of the x integer

@CHOOSE(*offset,list*)
>Returns the value or label of list represented by the offset

@CODE(*string*)
>Returns the code of the first character in the string

@COLS(*range*)
>Returns the number of columns in the specified range

@COORD(*worksheet,column,row,absolute*)
>Creates a cell reference according to the specified worksheet, column, and row

@COS(*x*)
>Calculates the cosine of x

@COUNT(*list*)
>Returns the number of cells that contain data in the specified list

@CTERM(*interest,future-value,present-value*)
>Calculates the periods an investment would take to reach the future-value earning the specified interest rate

@DATE(*year,month,day*)
>Calculates the date-number of the specified date

@DATEVALUE(*string*)
>Calculates the date-number for the specified date in the string

@DAVG(*input,field,criteria*)
>Calculates the average of a field in the specified criteria in a database

@DAY(*date-number*)
>Returns the day of the month specified by the date-number

@DCOUNT(*input,field,criteria*)
>Returns the number of nonblank cells in the field in the specified criteria in a database

@DDB(*cost,salvage,life,period*)
 Calculates the depreciation amount of an asset

@DGET(*input,field,criteria*)
 Returns the value or label in a field in the specified criteria in a
 database

@DMAX(*input,field,criteria*)
 Returns the largest value in a field in the specified criteria in a database

@DMIN(*input,field,criteria*)
 Returns the smallest value in a field in the specified criteria in a
 database

@DQUERY(*function,ext-arguments*)
 Accesses a function in an external database and uses the results of the
 function in a criteria range

@DSTD(*input,field,criteria*)
 Returns the standard deviation of a value in a field in the specified
 criteria in a database

@DSTDS(*input,field,criteria*)
 Returns the sample standard deviation of a value in a field in the
 specified criteria in a database

@DSUM(*input,field,criteria*)
 Returns sum of the values in a field in the specified criteria in a
 database

@D360(*start-date,end-date*)
 Calculates the number of days between the two specified dates

@DVAR(*input,field,criteria*)
 Returns the population variance of the values in a field in the specified criteria in a database

@DVARS(*input,field,criteria*)
> Returns the sample population variance of the values in a field in the specified criteria in a database

@ERR
> Returns the value of ERR

@EXACT(*string1,string2*)
> Compares two specified characters to see if they match

@EXP(*x*)
> Calculates the value of *e* (approx. 2.718282) to the power of x

@FALSE
> Returns the false value of 0

@FIND(*search-string,string,start-number*)
> Calculates the position of a string in the specified search-string and start-number

@FV(*payments,interest,term*)
> Calculates the future value of an investment based on the payments and interest

@HLOOKUP(*x,range,row-offset*)
> Returns the contents of a cell in the specified row in a horizontal lookup table

@HOUR(*time-number*)
> Returns the hour of the specified time-number

@IF(*condition,x,y*)
> Returns one of two values (x or y) after evaluating the condition

@INDEX(*range,column-offset,row-offset,worksheet-offset*)
> Returns the contents of a range specified by the column, row, and worksheet offset

@INFO(*attribute*)
> Returns information about the current 1-2-3 session

@INT(*x*)
   Returns the integer of x

@IRR(*guess,range*)
   Calculates the internal rate of return expected from an investment

@ISERR(*x*)
   Tests for ERR for the value x

@ISNA(*x*)
   Test for NA for the value x

@ISNUMBER(*x*)
   Tests x for a value

@ISRANGE(*range*)
   Tests range to see if it has a range name

@ISSTRING(*x*)
   Test x for a label or text enclosed in quotation marks

@LEFT(*string,n*)
   Returns the first n character in the specified string

@LENGTH(*string*)
   Returns the number of characters in the specified string

@LN(*x*)
   Calculates the natural logarithm (base e) of x

@LOG(*x*)
   Calculates the logarithm (base 10) of x

@LOWER(*string*)
   Converts all the letters in the specified string to lowercase

@MAX(*list*)
   Locates the largest value in the specified list

@MID(*string,start-number,n*)
>Returns the n character in the specified string starting at the start-number

@MIN(*list*)
>Locates the smallest value in the specified list

@MINUTE(*time-number*)
>Returns the minutes of the specified time-number

@MOD(*x,y*)
>Calculates the remainder of x/y

@MONTH(*date-number*)
>Returns the month of the specified date-number

@N(*range*)
>Returns the first cell's entry as a value

@NA
>Returns the value of NA (not available)

@NOW
>Calculates the number that corresponds to the date and time of the computer's clock

@NPV(*interest,range*)
>Calculates the net-present value at the specified range

@PI
>Returns the value of pie (3.14159265358979324)

@PMT(*principal,interest,term*)
>Calculates the payment amount on a loan at the specified principal, interest, and term of loan

@PROPER(*string*)
>Capitalizes the first character in each word in the specified string

@PV(*payment,interest,term*)
> Calculates the present value of an investment

@RAND
> Generates a random number between 0 and 1 up to 17 decimal places

@RATE(*future-value,present-value,term*)
> Returns the periodic interest rate needed to reach the specified future-value of an investment

@REPEAT(*string,n*)
> Repeats the specified string by the n value

@REPLACE(*original-string,start-number,n,new-string*)
> Replaces n characters in the original-string with the new-string beginning at the start-number

@RIGHT(*string,n*)
> Returns the last n characters in the specified string

@ROUND(*x,n*)
> Round the value of x to the nearest 10 by n

@ROW(*range*)
> Returns the number of rows in the specified range

@S(*range*)
> Returns the first entry in a cell of the specified range as a label

@SECOND(*time-number*)
> Returns the seconds specified by the time-number

@SHEETS(*range*)
> Returns the number of worksheets in the specified range

@SIN(*x*)
> Calculates the sine of angle x

@SLN(*cost,salvage,lift*)
> Calculates the straight-line depreciation allowance of an asset

@SOLVER(*query-string*)
> Returns a value that provides information on the status of Solver

@SQRT(*x*)
> Calculates the positive square root of x

@STD(*list*)
> Calculates the population standard deviation of the values in the specified list

@STDS(*list*)
> Calculates the sample standard deviation of the values in the specified list

@STRING(*x,n*)
> Converts the value x to a label with n decimal places

@SUM(*list*)
> Adds the values in the specified list

@SUMPRODUCT(*list*)
> Multiplies the values in corresponding cells in multiple ranges and sums up the products

@SYD(*cost,salvage,life,period*)
> Calculates the sum-of-the-years'-digits depreciation allowance of an asset

@TAN(*x*)
> Calculates the tangent of angle x

@TERM(*payments,interest,future-value*)
> Calculates the number of payments needed for an investment to reach the future-value at the specified interest rate

@TIME(*hour,minutes,seconds*)
> Calculates the time number of the specified hour, minutes, and seconds

@TIMEVALUE(*string*)
>   Calculates the time number of the time in the specified string

@TODAY
>   Calculates the date number of the current date

@TRIM(*string*)
>   Removes leading, trailing, and consecutive spaces from the specified string

@TRUE
>   Returns the value of 1

@UPPER(*string*)
>   Converts all of the letters in the specified string to uppercase

@VALUE(*string*)
>   Converts a number entered as a string to its corresponding value

@VAR(*list*)
>   Calculates the variance of values in the specified list

@VARS(*list*)
>   Calculates the sample population variance of the values in the specified list

@VDB(*cost,salvage,life,start-period,end-period,depreciation factor,switch*)
>   Calculates the depreciation allowance of an asset

@VLOOKUP(*x,range,column-offset*)
>   Returns the contents of a cell in the specified column in a vertical lookup table

@YEAR(*date-number*)
>   Returns the year of the specified date-number

This page unintentionally left blank.

Appendix C
Lotus 1-2-3 SmartIcons

This appendix lists the most-often-used Lotus 1-2-3 SmartIcons. You will
see the SmartIcon, the number of the palette you can find it on, and a
short description of what it does.

Icon	Palette	Enables You To
	1	Save your worksheet to a disk.
	1	Retrieve a worksheet file from disk.
	1	Read a file into memory after the current file.
	1	See three worksheets, stacked up.
	1	Move to the worksheet after this one.
	1	Move to the worksheet before this one.
	1	Calculate the sum of values in a range.
	1	Create, edit, or display a graph.
	1	Add your graph to the worksheet.
	1	Print a selected range of cells.
	1	Print the previous (or a specified) range.
	1	Add boldface to (or remove it from) a range.

continues

Icon	Palette	Enables You To
I	1	Add italics to (or clear them from) a range.
U	1	Add single underlining to (or remove it from) data in a range.
AA	1	Cycle through available fonts for a range.
?	1	Start the Help system.
U	2	Add double underlining to data in a range, or remove it.
$	2	Format values in a range as currency, or restore global format.
0,0	2	Format values in a range using comma format, or restore global format.
%	2	Format values in a range using percent format, or restore global format.
≣	2	Left-align a range's labels.
≣	2	Center a range's labels.
≣	2	Right-align a range's labels.
	3	Insert one or more rows above the highlighted rows.
	3	Insert one or more columns to the left of the highlighted column.
	3	Delete all rows in the highlighted range.
	3	Delete all columns in the highlighted range.
A↓Z	3	Sort a database in ascending order; current column is the sort key.

Icon	Palette	Enables You To
	3	Sort a database in descending order; current column is the sort key.
	4	Move cell pointer left one cell.
	4	Move cell pointer right one cell.
	4	Move cell pointer up one cell.
	4	Move cell pointer down one cell.
	4	Move cell pointer to upper left corner of worksheet.
	4	Move cell pointer to lower right corner of worksheet.
	5	Move cell pointer to a cell you specify.
	5	Find or replace characters in a range's labels and formulas.
	5	Copy highlighted range to a range you specify.
	5	Move highlighted range to a range you specify.
	5	Cancel previous action or command if Undo feature is on.
	5	Erase highlighted range.
	6	Display current graph.
	7	Select and run a macro.
	7	Add an icon to your custom palette.

continues

Icon	Palette	Enables You To
	7	Remove an icon from your custom palette.
	7	Rearrange icons on custom palettes.

Glossary

Speak Like a Geek: The Complete Archives

Absolute cell address   An address that specifies a fixed worksheet location.

Add-in   A program that works together with 1-2-3 to provide additional features.

AND operator   When searching a database on two criteria, the AND operator specifies that a record will be considered a match only if *both* criteria are met.

Argument   Information that tells a function what data to work with.

Axis scale   The maximum and minimum values displayed on a graph's axis.

Category data   Data that is represented by labels in the worksheet.

Cell address   A letter-number combination that specifies the location of a worksheet cell by the letter of its column and number of its row.

Column width   The number of default-size characters that will fit in a column.

Criteria   A set of rules, or patterns, that specify which records in a database table to match. (Note: "criteria" is plural; the singular is "criterion.")

Criteria range   A worksheet range in which you enter search criteria for finding records in a database table.

Current graph   The graph that was most recently displayed.

Database   A collection of data items that all have the same structure, but each one contains different information.

Date serial number   The number of days between January 1, 1900 and the current date.

Default directory   The directory where 1-2-3 keeps worksheet files (unless you tell it otherwise).

Display mode   The way a computer program displays things on the screen. Many programs, including 1-2-3, have two or more display modes.

DOS Prompt   An on-screen prompt indicating that your computer is ready to accept a command. It usually looks something like C:\> or C:>.

Drop shadow   A darker area below and to the right of a cell or range, producing the illusion of a shadow.

ERR   1-2-3 displays this message in a worksheet cell that contains a formula that cannot be evaluated.

Exponentiation   Raising a number to a power. For example, 2^3 means "two to the third power," or 2*2*2.

Field   An item of information contained in each database record.

Field names   Unique names that identify the fields in a database table.

File   A place on a disk where information, such as a worksheet, is stored.

Font attributes   Characteristics of (and changes to) the way text is displayed, including boldface, underlining, and italics.

Font set   A set of eight fonts available for use in a worksheet.

Footer   A line of text printed at the bottom of every page in a report.

Formula   An instruction that tells 1-2-3 to combine or manipulate numbers in a certain way, such as adding or subtracting them.

Frame   The border at the top and left edges of the worksheet, where the column letters and row numbers are displayed, is called the *worksheet frame*.

Free cell   In POINT mode, the cell that marks the movable corner of the highlighted range.

Function   A formula that is built into 1-2-3. They are sometimes called *"at" functions* because their names all start with the "at" symbol (@): @SUM, @ROUND, etc.

Header   A line of text printed at the top of every page in a report.

Label prefix character   One of three special characters (' " and ^) that mark a cell entry as a label, and tell 1-2-3 how to align the label in the cell.

Landscape orientation   The long edge of the paper is horizontal when printing.

Leading zero   A zero displayed before the decimal point for numbers between 1 and –1: for example, 0.125.

Legend   A key that identifies a graph's data ranges by color, symbol, or hatch pattern.

Margin   Blank space between the edge of the page and the printed area.

Mixed cell address   A cell address where some of the components (worksheet letter, column letter, and row number) are absolute and some are relative.

Named style   A collection of WYSIWYG formats that has been assigned a name.

Numeric data   Data that is represented by numbers, or *values*, in the worksheet.

On line   A printer is said to be "on line" when it is ready to print.

On-line   Directly available to you on your computer while you are working.

Operator precedence   The order in which 1-2-3 evaluates (that is, makes use of) arithmetic operators in a formula.

OR operator   When searching a database on two criteria, the OR operator specifies that a record will be considered a match if either one (or both) of the criteria are met.

Page break   A command that instructs 1-2-3 to start a new page at a particular row or column when printing. The resulting division between pages is also called a page break.

Point   A unit of measure used for fonts and for row heights. One point equals 1/72 of an inch.

Point mode   A worksheet mode that permits you, when entering a command that operates on a range, to "point out" the range by moving the cell pointer.

Portrait orientation   The long edge of the paper is vertical when printing.

Range   A rectangular group of one or more worksheet cells that is treated as a unit.

Record   One complete database entry.

Relative cell address   An address that specifies a location relative to the cell containing the formula.

Retrieve   To load a worksheet from disk into 1-2-3 for further editing.

Selection indicators   Small filled squares displayed on selected objects in the graph editing window.

Sort key   A database field that is used to order records when the database is sorted.

Thousands separators   Commas placed every third digit in large numbers, such as 1,000,000.

Trailing zeros   One or more zeros placed at the end of a decimal number to fill out the specified number of decimal places: for example, 1.5000.

Typeface   A particular design for printed and displayed characters.

Wild card characters   When entering criteria for /Data Find operations, * and ? are wild card characters that match any one character (?) or any group of characters (*).

WYSIWYG   Pronounced "whizzy-wig," an acronym for What You See Is What You Get, describing a computer program in which the display on the screen looks essentially the same as printed output. Also the name of a 1-2-3 add-in program that provides WYSIWYG capabilities.

This page unintentionally left blank.

Index

Symbols

– (minus sign)
  in numbers, 23
  subtraction operator, 99
(pound sign) in headers and
  footers, 150-151
$ (dollar sign)
  absolute cell addresses, 119
  in numbers, 24
& (concatenation) operator, 102
, (comma), numeric format, 131
' (left-aligned) prefix character, 25
() (parentheses) in functions, 109
" (right-aligned) prefix character,
  25
* (asterisk)
  multiplication operator, 99
  rows of, 75
  wild card character, searching
    with, 213-214

+ (addition) operator, 99
. (period key) anchoring
  pointer, 62
→ key
  data query navigation, 219
  EDIT mode, 28
  file retrieval lists, 52
  Help system, 43
  worksheet navigation, 20
↓ key
  data query navigation, 219
  EDIT mode, 28
  Help system, 43
  worksheet navigation, 20
/ character
  division operator, 99
  main 1-2-3 menu, 3
< (less than) operator, 214-215
<= (less than or equal to)
  operator, 214
<> (not equal to) operator, 214

A

G

More Fun Learning from Alpha Books!

If you enjoyed
The Complete Idiot's Guide to Windows,
then check out these books!

**For more information
or to place an order, call**

1-800-428-5331

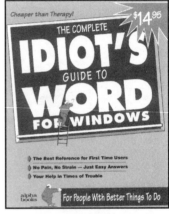

**The Complete Idiot's Guide
to PCs**
ISBN: 1-56761-168-0
Softbound, $14.95 USA

**The Complete Idiot's Guide
to Word for Windows**
ISBN: 1-56761-174-5
Softbound, $14.95 USA

**The Complete Idiot's Guide
to DOS**
ISBN: 1-56761-169-9
Softbound, $14.95 USA